THIS
IS
YOUR
MOTHER

A Memoir

Erika J. Simpson

SCRIBNER

New York   Amsterdam/Antwerp

London   Toronto   Sydney/Melbourne   New Delhi

Scribner
An Imprint of Simon & Schuster, LLC
1230 Avenue of the Americas
New York, NY 10020

The "Exodus" chapter has been adapted from material previously published in *The Audacity* (under the title "If You Ever Find Yourself").

First Scribner hardcover edition May 2025

SCRIBNER and design are trademarks of Simon & Schuster, LLC

Simon & Schuster strongly believes in freedom of expression and stands against censorship in all its forms. For more information, visit BooksBelong.com.

For information about special discounts for bulk purchases, please contact Simon & Schuster Special Sales at 1-866-506-1949 or business@simonandschuster.com.

The Simon & Schuster Speakers Bureau can bring authors to your live event. For more information or to book an event, contact the Simon & Schuster Speakers Bureau at 1-866-248-3049 or visit our website at www.simonspeakers.com.

Interior design by Kathryn A. Kenney-Peterson

Manufactured in the United States of America

10 9 8 7 6 5 4 3 2 1

Library of Congress Cataloging-in-Publication Data has been applied for.

ISBN 978-1-6680-2403-4
ISBN 978-1-6680-2405-8 (ebook)

For my sister

THIS
IS
YOUR
MOTHER

PART ONE

Genesis

Imagine this is your mother. Sallie Carol. Daughter of share-croppers. Middle of ten. She's a June Gemini, inquisitive and playful, so sensitive she cries before the switch reaches her legs. She pretends to be the teacher in games of schoolhouse, leads the neighborhood kids on adventures along the creek, and most of all she yearns for a life beyond the fields of North Carolina.

The Wizard of Oz premieres in color during her childhood, a magic that lingers in the corners of her eyes well into her fifties. How a small-town girl can wish hard enough to leave home and find herself in a whimsical world with new friends and opportunities. She performs "The Impossible Dream" by The Temptations in her high school talent show, and even though she can't sing, she takes home the second-place trophy. A moment that proves to her all things are possible if you believe in yourself enough.

Out of all her mama's children she's the sickly one—the runt, she'd say, always suffering from an ailment. One day she collapses beside the house with a ruptured appendix. Her brother finds her unconscious body in the nick of time and she goes on to hold a hunger for life, faith in miracles.

She finishes high school and excels in college, begins a career teaching science straight after. She dates a boy her parents don't like, Steven Simpson, and impassioned with love, they marry without approval. Three years later they have a child, Samantha Novella. Marriage and motherhood are rewarding, but Sallie's first love is still education. She goes back to school for her master's degree, creating tension with her man over priorities. She works; her husband cheats. A tumor develops in her brain. He stays through the sickness but is unfaithful during health. Sallie files for divorce.

She indulges in one last night with the man she married on the occasion of his birthday and they accidentally beget you, their second child. A baby Sallie births despite the separation and the doctor's warning that the pressure paired with her brain tumor would kill her. She wants Samantha to have someone, long after Daddy leaves and Mommy passes. The baby is a miracle and so is she, surviving the delivery and later surgery to remove the tumor. Sallie interprets God's grace to mean that there's a calling on her life and dedicates herself to guiding others.

While attending an educators' conference, she hears a charismatic speaker named Henry Orville Braddock from Atlanta. The clinical psychologist inspires her to found her own business, Freedom Peace, Inc., where she'll heal the wounded through counseling sessions and seminars. A project that combines her passions for education, faith, and connection. She departs from North Carolina to Atlanta, thirsty for a city she can actualize in, and leaves you and your sister with her brother's family while she gets things situated in Atlanta.

Sallie maintains a decent apartment and a modest office, teaching science by day and working on her business at night, but the adjustment for a single-income family in a new city is not without its challenges. She chooses her dream over the day-to-day, investing in Freedom Peace instead of paying rent. Evictions come easy. You and your sister shift with her from apartments to hotels while her recurring sickness becomes sibling in its incessant presence. She has no money, no safety net aside from her brothers' and sisters' Western Union transfers. She relies on her instincts and charisma, her drive, and, above all, her God. And when you leave home to create your own future, she presses on, alone in the city she chose for herself.

August
2013

Your phone vibrates against the floor. Someone's calling. It could be your mother, but it's after 7:00 pm. Usually she calls first thing in the morning while she's running errands in Decatur, Georgia, and the sun is barely up in Chicago. The phone screen shows Aunt Mattie from Greensboro. Unusual. She's more of an afternoon caller. You brace yourself.

She called to tell you what your mother would not: The cancer is back. This time it's in your mother's blood and all over her spine. The doctors say she has two months to live.

Before this, you were flipping through your high school yearbook, reminiscing, trying not to think about everything you lost or what your mother continues to lose. Growing up, you imagined yourself on stage by now, but the only acting you do is a friendly tone for the customers at the call center. It's okay. You're maintaining your life, your two black cats, and the wood-walled apartment you call home. You've made friends in the city to call family. The past feels further away every day.

What should you do with the information you've been given?

While you're avoiding memories of toys lost to eviction, your mother's life could be next. You decide not to believe it. She's been given diagnoses before: a brain tumor when you were born, ovarian cancer when you were six, breast cancer when you were in fourth grade and again your junior year of high school. This is always happening. The diagnosis. The predicted life expectancy. An endless loop of psychological torture taunting your family to guess when she will go. She went to the doctor every week and took pills every morning and sang her gospel songs while she cooked breakfast. Somehow she's still alive.

You tell your aunt it will be fine. The sentence feels stale in your mouth. She insists you need to understand the gravity of the situation this time. Your mama probably hasn't told you because she wants to be strong, but you must be prepared for the worst. Okay, you say. The both of you sit in silence on the phone. You wonder if your sister knows.

Aunt Mattie's background is quiet. The absence of the sound of sizzling grease or running dishwater is deafening. You imagine her sitting in the dark of the den, waiting for you to speak. You tell her you'll call your mother, then hang up.

You wish phones were like they used to be so you could dial one rotary number at a time. But she's only a button away. There's hardly a moment to collect yourself.

When she answers, you hear wind behind her words. She's hustling from the train to the bus. She says she was running errands. She says she has no money for a hotel tonight, but the Lord will make a way. She says the women at the post office were playing games, purposefully making things harder for her. She didn't pay the forty-three dollars for her PO box, and they wouldn't give her the mail, but she thinks she has a check coming. All of this sounds normal, for her, and you don't want to bring up the cancer. You want it to be her cross to bear so you can ignore her calls at six in the morning without guilt. But time is limited. "I talked to Aunt Mattie," you tell her.

The wind somehow ceases to blow and everything on your mother's end goes silent. She knows what you're trying to ask. But she wants things to stay normal too.

You're forced to continue. "She says the cancer came back. She says you only have two months to live."

Her voice races through the receiver, rough and close, grabbing you by the shoulders. You haven't been to Decatur, Georgia, in over a year, yet you can still feel her fingers on your upper arms as she speaks.

"*Listen!*" she spits into the phone, "*I haven't gone nowhere yet, have I? The Lord been keeping me here for a reason, right? So how some doctor gon' tell me when to die? Mama gon' be all right. You hear me? Your mama gonna live.*"

A bus honks in the background, breaking the spell. You nod your head yes and you can tell that she knows this. You're crying, and she knows this too. She calls you her baby girl and says that you shouldn't worry. She'll be okay. Mama is okay. She says she has to catch the train. But you will talk again soon, and you will not worry. You take the phone away from your ear.

Your mother has two months to live. You know because she grabbed you by the shoulders with her voice and she's never done that before.

Exodus

If your mother is a devout Christian, like mine, she'll raise you mostly by faith, which entails a great deal of hustling to make it to the next blessing. While Mama studied her Bible, I studied her, making scriptures from the ways she kept us afloat.

Book of Sallie Carol 1:2: The only things that matter, and the order of their importance, are food and rent. Don't pay no bill before you've eaten. Because how you look sitting around with all the lights on but nothing to eat? You can ignore any gas, electric, or water bills that come in a white envelope. Those are nudges. Once you get a red letter or a final notice, call Customer Service.

My mama said the best phone representatives were women with southern accents thicker than ours. Those are the ones you tell your story to when you need an extension on the bills. As a single mother, she sure didn't have money, but she always had her story. I'd sit quiet beside her while the voice on the house phone rattled off three-digit numbers we owed. Mama's face would frown up like she could be seen, and she'd tell them how her mother died a couple months ago, and how her husband left her with two babies, and how she couldn't get a steady job. The operator would let her put twenty dollars down and we'd live to heat the house another day.

It's interesting because the first rule of being broke is not to let anyone know you're broke. But a good sob story has value in it if you gain favor instead of sympathy from telling it. A favor being a waived bill or a free meal, because remember: you've got to eat sooner than you've got to pay the rent.

Book of Sallie Carol 6:6: If you've got nothing else, have faith. Not just figuratively, but literally. When you're hungry, turn to the church for a handout. They can't turn you away or they aren't disciples of Christ.

You'll learn quickly, though, that the bounty isn't plentiful enough to endure the heavenly sisters swarming around your raggedy apartment. Whenever we asked for help from the church, Mama would clean the tables and sweep the floors and tell me and Samantha to look hungry but not starved. Appreciative but not desperate. The church ladies loved to gossip. Everyone knew that from the extra hour they spent whispering in the parking lot after the sermon. The sisters insisted on dropping the box of food off inside. They'd lightly touch the counters with a prayer hand and strut around the kitchen like the Make-A-Wish Foundation for bringing canned peas, ramen noodles, and powdered milk. Mama knew a description of our place would pass through the congregation afterward. But you do what you gotta do to eat. They never even brought snacks. Just nonperishables and prayer.

The worst part is that afterward you have to come to church at least two more Sundays in a row looking thankful. Extra points if you give a testimony and pass out while you're clapping and screaming, *Thank you, Jesus! Thank you, holy saints, for blessing us!* while the congregation get to shouting, *Amen! Amen!*

You'll still be broke on Monday morning.

Another way to eat is with **reverse Robin Hooding**, in which you challenge the poor to give to the poor if they're working for the rich. This trick works best at places with cafeteria-style serving. You'll be used to sharing your mother's shame, but this one feels particularly embarrassing. This is the one where you've got to look like a child starving in a third-world country on command and you pray no one's behind you in line.

I stood like a sad prop as my mama asked the cashier at JJ's to slide a hot plate of fish and greens to us for free. She had him pile the to-go plate up nice and big with fried okra, creamy mac and cheese, and an extra catfish fillet before admitting we had no money to pay for it. "My babies haven't eaten all day," she pleaded. I didn't look at my older sister and she didn't look at me. We were both pretending we didn't know each other and that we didn't exist. The cashier didn't look at Mama as he slid the plate toward us on the counter. We lived to eat another meal.

When you can't take sporadic food any longer, or the feeling that everyone at church knows your business, or the look in a teenage cashier's eyes when they realize you have absolutely nothing, you can **take the bus down to the family aid office and apply for food stamps**. Food stamps are the most stable and humiliating option. Nowadays they give out plastic debit cards with a picture of your state on the front so you remember who's footing the bill. But back then, the caseworkers would hand you what looked like Monopoly money: bright Easter-colored food vouchers representing ones, fives, tens, and twenties. Oranges and pinks loud enough to be heard. Bright enough to tell everybody in line behind you that you're on government aid and your daddy left your mama for a white woman and now she can't even support herself or the babies she laid down to have.

If you need money for more than food and don't wanna carry around play-play money, you could do like Mama and flip it. Mama could sell fifty dollars' worth of food stamps for twenty-five dollars' worth of real cash to teachers she subbed with, her post office lady friends, or sisters from church. It was a beautiful hustle. We got to have money for bus fare and replacement clothes, and they got to have food stamps without *having* food stamps. Nobody wanted to be the black family on welfare.

Book of Sallie Carol 2:6: Conceal what's real. Parade your poverty only for people who can help, never for those who will judge you like the church ladies. If you're ever broke during grade school, you'll learn that your mama's worried about rent while your peers are worried about designer clothes.

Kids at my school flashed Sean Jean and Baby Phat paired with fresh Timberland boots, name brands that meant *their* mamas weren't worried about anything. The seventh-grade boys would clutch their belt buckles like they worked somewhere. Like they didn't just beg their mamas in the mall over the summer. My mama told me the truth: "We ain't got it like that." So I got regular clothes from T.J. Maxx and Walmart.

Book of Sallie Carol 2:12: Buy staples, not statements. Only rich people make statements. Buy staples you can wear a few times without being noticed. A good pair of jeans and a nice pair of khakis. A black shirt, a white shirt, and one with a collar. Mama said to always keep your jacket and your shoes nice, since that's what catches people's eyes first, though we rarely had money to replace my sneakers before the soles started talking. Lay low. If you don't have anything, don't flaunt anything.

I'd seen baby Negroes tear a girl apart because the stitching on her FUBU dress looked off. They'd surrounded another boy like a pack of hyenas over his shoes. They howled up at the tile ceilings, cackling with their tongues hanging out until he crumpled within himself. "Boy, I thought them were Air Force Ones! He rockin' Skechers!" If you can't afford the real thing don't even bother with something resembling. That's all you'll look like, something resembling. Stick to plain black shoes from Walmart.

You can talk your way out of paying bills and con your way into some food stamps. You can hide that you're poor in public as long as you can shower, but you can't hide an eviction.

If it's the first of the month and you can't afford the rent, you can call the landlord and let them know you need more time. Asking is better than silence, unless you've been late on the rent before. Don't panic yet.

Book of Sallie Carol 2:7: The money isn't due, due until the fifth of the month. Landlords can't legally evict a nonpaying tenant until the third month. If you really don't have it—and this will get a little awkward with daily notices and letters—but if you really don't have them people's money, you have at least two full months to try to raise it.

Mama did well teaching public school unless she was into it with whoever was the principal. At one school she challenged the man's morals when he told her to bump grades for a few failing white kids whose parents had donated money. He threatened to fire her if she didn't comply. She told that white man, "Mother fuck you," and he kept his promise.

The last check from that job withered away into nothing after food, partial rent, clothes, car payments, partial bills, and credit card debt. We moved from the apartments with shiny new appliances and front-facing balconies and into ones with fake entrance gates that always hung pathetically open. Where the units themselves masked endless roaches, scattering across the counters and from under the trash can no matter how much we cleaned. Substitute-teaching jobs came fewer and further between for Mama and soon her credit score couldn't even get us the dirty brick flat-level apartments in the cloudy part of town.

Once my aunts and uncles got tired of Mama calling for Western Union money wires and the child support checks from the father I never met dried up, evictions came one after the other.

If you're more than three months behind on rent in an apartment building, make sure someone is always home. Because as soon as the office manager peeps you heading to the grocery store, they'll violently throw your things into the street. They'll throw your clothes out still on the hangers; the whole dresser with panties leaking out the drawers; books, pots, and photo albums, right onto the sidewalk, right in front of where you park your car every day, so everybody knows the stuff is yours. The worst part of this eviction isn't that the neighbors will know how broke your family is but that the very same neighbors will take your furniture if you aren't back fast enough. TV sets and coffee tables disappear the quickest, but you'll never find out who took your stuff since you're banished from the complex now. You'll probably have to change schools again too, depending on how far away the next apartment complex is. Another perk of laying low at school is that you don't have to miss anybody or explain why your family has to up and leave.

Whenever we got evicted, we'd rent a U-Haul if Mama could afford it, or just cram our sentimentals into the backseat and try to find somewhere to stay before the eviction hit her credit report. I'd sit in the back with boxes piled up around me and on my lap, trying not to let Mama see me cry over lost Goosebumps books or Barbie dolls. That's just how it goes. We stayed in rotating apartments in three-month intervals and then seedy rent-by-the-week motels after Mama's credit report started hissing with venom.

Book of Sallie Carol 4:2: *Avoid motels if you can. Motels are the easiest to get evicted from.* You have to secure the thirty-five-dollar daily fee to keep the door clicking open, which sounds cheap but totals more than rent on a house after a month. The roadside motels were slimy-looking haunts with stiff comforters on the beds and lamp lighting that gave everything a yellow teeth stain kinda vibe. When you're living in a motel because your mama hasn't found a good job yet, a good tip is to leave twenty minutes earlier on school mornings and walk over to the bus stop by the fancy apartments down the street. Mama said if people thought we weren't doing so well, The State could take me away from her, so remember not to tell anybody our business. Keep up appearances. **Book of Sallie Carol 2:6** again—*conceal.*

There were other families staying in those motels too, but somehow we never knew faces or names. Nobody looked anybody in the eyes at 6:30 in the morning. Mamas waved goodbye to kids. We ran across the parking lot like the roaches scattering out, heading toward a bus stop that wouldn't make a comment on our lives.

One Sunday, when we got back from begging the Lord for

money at church, our motel door wouldn't open. The motel eviction is the worst because they lock your stuff *inside* when you don't pay and they won't let you back in unless you pay within twenty-four hours.

I wailed for my favorite teddy bear, the last good item I had left after several evictions. Mama rushed me into the front office for the clerk to see. "You'd let a baby cry over a few dollars?" She convinced him to let us in for just a moment, and I stood moaning and yanking on my pigtails beside the manager while Mama filled up three big garbage bags with our things. She handed me the brown plush teddy in front of him so he could focus on her baby smiling and not on how we were getting our stuff without paying. I didn't feel like a baby anymore. But I definitely felt helpless.

If you ever find yourself with a credit score too low to say out loud, and a mountain of debt, remember ***Book of Sallie Carol 1:1: Dream big. Beyond limitations, big.*** It's one of the most important of Mama's beliefs because ***dreaming reshapes your reality***. When you're passionate about something, follow through on it. Even if you fail, at least you tried, which is success in and of itself.

Mama kept Freedom Peace running with her substitute-teaching money. She wanted to use her skills to help people, as if we hadn't just moved into a motel indefinitely. I felt stuck in my mother's struggle story and started strategizing on how I could break the cycle of poverty.

While Mama was busy trying to find an Office Depot associate to show her how to print her business brochure so it folded correctly, something caught my eye above the staplers. A flyer on the bulletin board: *Looking for charismatic kids to join the cast of a new local children's show! Auditions to be held at Decatur Library,*

Saturday @ noon. I'd seen the kids dancing in a random studio on *ZOOM*. This could be it. Mama didn't hesitate when I showed her.

She had me wear khaki pants and a hot pink shirt, braided the top of my hair, and then curled the back. When we got to the library, an older white man dressed in jeans and a vest like we were going on safari greeted us out front. A big camera hung around his neck and a tripod rested over his shoulder. He shook Mama's hand and told us he had reserved one of the quiet reading rooms and that she should wait outside while we filmed. That made me nervous. In eight years of my life, I had never been alone with an adult man. Never hugged my father. Never prayed one-on-one with the pastor. I figured I had never been touched or beaten because Mama never had a man around me.

Nevertheless, Mama nodded reassuringly and left me to be filmed. The man pointed his camera at me. He said there were no lines, just scenarios. He told me to say my name and after I said it loud and clear I added, "Are all my friends ready to play?" He ate it up. I gave him a blockbuster kid performance, holding up books and talking about reading on rainy days, dramatically pouting before grinning big. The producer loved everything I did. He told Mama she had a little star on her hands, and we left full of hope, awaiting his follow-up phone call. It crushed me when we never heard back. I wanted to change the scripture to *Never have hope; it'll kill you when the plans fall through*, but Mama would say that's what the devil wants, to make you feel defeated. Someone told me I was a star. That was confirmation enough.

No matter our collective or separate efforts for forward momentum, we had to find contentment in the present. We had each other if ever we had nothing else. ***Book of Sallie Carol 3:3: Home still feels like home, when you're surviving together.*** Because if you think where you're living is bad, not being around your kin-folk would be even worse.

One year, Mama claimed to have found a good deal on a house. My sister and I ingested this information with caution. Mama said the lady gave a generously low offer on the monthly rent. But once we walked up the dirt and gravel path to the house, we found ourselves outside a dingy white single-story shack, paint chipping everywhere. I did what I do best and caged my disappointment. It had to be better than staying in a hotel.

Each room of the house was a further disappointment. There was no refrigerator in the kitchen. There were two bedrooms, but one had a slant because the floor was sinking into the ground. In the bathroom, there was no showerhead and the toilet wouldn't flush unless you lifted the top off the commode and pulled the chain. Mama put a brave face on and told us that we had ourselves a fixer-upper.

The vibe in the house never quite felt right, but we didn't have money to go anywhere else, or even to pay the next month's rent, so we tried to remain grateful. A strange odor began to fill the house, but it wasn't from the food. Upon closer inspection, Mama discovered a dead squirrel beneath the window, flies hovering over the body.

When we were leaving to catch the buses to school, we found thumbtacks and rusted nails littered all over the front porch, noticed only after Mama howled in pain from stepping on one. There were nights I'd be watching television in the den and swear I saw a shadow run past my peripheral.

Despite my supernatural suspicions, it turned out the evil spirit was the landlady. When Mama confronted the woman, she confirmed it was her like a Scooby-Doo bandit. She was pissed Mama hadn't paid her gracefully low rent for two months and demanded we pay or leave. Mama packed us up. We weren't paying back rent on a shack. She said we were children of God, that we were blessed and highly favored, despite circumstance. We'd made the best of it as long as possible. We could make the best of something else.

Book of Sallie Carol 6:12: There are no neat, happy endings, only the next step in the journey. It's easy to imagine that after you've suffered a trial or hardship, next you'll be transformed like Cinderella, swept from the basement to the castle, the bad times behind you. But it's not always the case. Sometimes the only transformation is inside you.

We headed back to a hotel. It wouldn't be long before we'd all be split up. Situations like that conditioned me to not have faith at all. Or worse, not have hope. But hope is like a dream in that it helps you survive. And at least having hope is free. Remember that like commandment.

September

You have trouble sleeping at night. There are too many variables. It's been one month since the health reveal, which means there's only one month left. You scroll aimlessly through the pictures and texts on your phone until your eyeballs ache. Anything not to think of where your mother could be tonight. Or how she is. She said she would be all right. Just as you're about to drift to sleep, your cell phone buzzes.

It's her.

What's worse, knowing or not knowing? You never could decide. You put the cell phone under your pillow. The vibrations stop. You breathe shallow breaths as if you're asleep, putting on an act for a woman who's thousands of miles away. The vibrations start again. You answer.

Her voice cuts through the silence resting in your ears, and you are suddenly where she is and as panicked as she feels.

"Hello? Are you there? They put me out. I don't know where to go. The hotel manager put my stuff outside the room. I'm sick. My feet are swollen so big it hurts to walk and I feel like I can't breathe. I don't know where to go."

You tell your mother to slow down. Your heart aches in that way it does when someone you love is hurt or has hurt you. You feel both now—she is hurting and she's hurting you because you can't help. All you can do is know. You're practically her only confidant. Samantha rarely answers her calls, and the two of you rarely discuss it. Mama's sisters and brothers stopped sending money after a decade of wiring hundred-dollar bills to Atlanta, her needs never fully satisfied. It is mostly you now, alone with your mother, and it's suffocating.

"It's two o'clock in the morning here. And I have all my stuff. The hotel manager was laughing. I'm a child of God. He knows I'm sick and he still went through with this. I just need one hundred and eighty dollars. Do you have that? It's one-thirty for the night, but for fifty dollars more I can stay for three days. If I can stay for three days I have time to figure something else out. It's so cold out here, baby. Mommy's in so much pain. I just want to rest, Lord."

You hear the labored breaths she takes between sentences. It sounds like she's tearing up from the stress, which causes your stomach to twist and contort violently. Here you are: resting comfortably in a queen-size bed, in a heated apartment, basic luxuries that your mother doesn't have. What do you do? There's $253 in your bank account. Enough to buy her a room for three more nights, leaving you with $73. The $65 phone bill is due in two days. That would leave you $8 to eat with for the next week and a half. Samantha would say giving her 70 percent of the money you made stocking shelves at Target does not sound smart.

But sending the money would feel good. You'll be her personal hero, as heavy as that is for a daughter to be for a mother. What's a week of poverty to give your sick mother a good night's sleep?

Samantha will sit in silence on the phone when you tell her what you've done. She'll think you haven't learned from the two thousand dollars of credit card debt Mama racked up in her name. Maybe you're naive. Or maybe just softhearted.

"Baby, are you there? Do you have anything, anything at all, you can send to help? Even ten dollars. Do you have ten dollars you can send so I can at least get something to eat? I'm so tired, baby. Sometimes I ask God why he won't just let me die."

She is in full tears now. Your body shakes beneath the covers as you search for what to say. If you don't send her the money she'll have nowhere to go! She'll walk Memorial Drive until a bus comes, no doubt with two heavy suitcases dragging behind her. She's fifty-six years old for Christ's sake! Her knees are bad from playing basketball in her youth, coaching cheerleaders in her twenties. Are you a bad person if you choose not to send it? She has stage four cancer! *Give her the money—give it to her!* What do you have to say for yourself? What are you going to tell her?

"Hello? Are you there? Please talk to me, child; I ain't got nobody else."

You tell her you are here. That you are listening. She goes quiet, waiting for your answer, but you're afraid. "I don't have it, Mama. I can't afford to send anything or my bills won't get paid." *Give it to her!* Why won't you just give it to her?

"You can't spare twenty dollars, baby? I'm just so tired. Lord knows I'm so tired."

How did she get to this place? Why is she bringing you with her? *Just send her something.* There's a Western Union near your job. There's always a bill to put off. **Book of Sallie Carol 1:2.** "I can send you forty dollars in the morning. But that's all I can spare."

"Thank you, baby. You always look out for Mommy. I'm at a bus stop right now. Just sitting with my stuff. I have important papers in here. I know the devil will do anything to take me out. But he won't win. You got to stay strong for me, baby. It's you and me against the world."

She sounds like she is drifting off and it scares you.

"You have to keep reaching out for me. Ask your friends if they have anything they can spare. You could take up a collection. If ten of your friends . . . that's a hundred dollars right there. Just keep the faith, baby. Everything is gonna be all right. One day I'ma have more money than I can count and people gonna wish they had helped."

The voice screaming for you to help subsides, and a sprinkle of relief calms your stomach. She is still talking. Despite wanting to hang up, you keep listening. This could be her last month. Mama always quoted Shirley Caesar songs about cherishing your mama and told you and Samantha that you'd miss her when she was gone.

You tell her that she should go to the hospital, mimicking the things she's taught you. ***Book of Sallie Carol 4:3: Find a communal space to blend into.*** Megastores, libraries, hospitals. Grady Memorial Hospital's open twenty-four hours a day and they can check on her feet. She agrees to this. It will give her somewhere to be until the morning. She sees a bus coming that can get her to the train station to head to Grady. Good. You'll know where she is for the night.

"I love you."

"I love you too." Exhaustion overcomes your senses and you drift to sleep. You dream you find your mother's body in your bed, bundled up like a newborn. It's up to you to unswaddle her.

You wake up to the front door opening and closing with a soft click. Your roommate's been dancing in Boystown for so long that there's only a couple hours before your mutual shifts at Target. You hope you don't have to cover the rent again. You both get the same $480 check to stretch. Plus your roommate doesn't have a mom like yours. Your phone screen lights up with two missed calls and two voicemails from your mother; no doubt the night before has been an ordeal. You'll head to Western Union before work. Pay your tithes and offerings.

1998

We were living in a hotel called Aloha Motor Inn in Decatur, Georgia, which had tacky tropical leaf wallpaper and ugly patterned carpet. Mama got my sister and me up early for a Walmart run. The hotel doors would lock us out for nonpayment at 11:00 am, so we had to move quick. She was being unusually quiet, Mama. No complaints about the hotel bill or how we were going to get Samantha to West Georgia by 3:00 pm. Sister was so smart she got selected for a program where high school seniors do their final year at the college for additional credits. We couldn't let our lives mess this opportunity up.

Mama kept a pleasant poker face in Walmart, telling my sister to grab toiletries and a couple new shirts and notebooks for the school year. She didn't even mention the prices. Highly suspicious. As soon as we got back to the room, she told us to pack up our book bags and fold whatever couldn't fit into a trash bag for transport, then she called a cab.

A nervous tension filled the car for the whole hour-long ride. The driver kept asking questions: "She's a smart girl, huh? Is that all your stuff? Why you taking a cab?" He kept looking up at

Mama through the rearview mirror. Evaluating. My sister and I sat silent. I was in the middle, bumping and sliding with every turn. Wondering if Mama had another child support check or Western Union she hadn't told us about. But she would have said if she did. She damn sure always said if she didn't. There wasn't so much as a *God will make a way* out of her.

We pulled up to the registration office, got out, and stood blinking at each other beside the car while the driver sat staring forward. Parents and students milled around us for their normal drop-off day. Mama grinned big and hugged Samantha tight. There wasn't any seeing her dorm room or walking around on campus. Mama told the man by way of telling Samantha that we had to get right back to the city, so she was going to do a round-trip ride with the cabbie. Samantha waved feebly goodbye as Mama and I popped into the backseat, then walked inside with her backpack and trash bag, disappearing into the crowd of stable families. My brain scrambled to piece together the plan.

The cabbie was looking at Mama real hard in the rearview now. Asking more questions: "You don't just want to pay out? You didn't want to stay to see her off? Where you rushing back to?"

Mama started spieling about her counseling business and drug and alcohol abuse and how more than four drinks a week was alcoholism, and she kept going until the man stopped looking at her and focused on the road. His knuckles gripped the steering wheel. An hour back to the city. The numbers on his meter were already at $175 and they kept ticking. Above all else, we had checked out of the hotel this morning, so I wasn't even sure where Mama would have him drop us off. We had everything on us, at least, so we wouldn't have to pull up to our stuff locked inside a room or anything.

When the cab got back into the city, Mama feigned remembering something: "You know what? Drop us off at the Walmart; I need a few things." He looked at us suspiciously. He had already peeped the pack job. My mousy demeanor. We didn't have time to drop a kid off at precollege but had time for a Walmart run? Unlikely. He stopped the cab right in front of the entrance, which made my stomach hurt even more because it felt like we were about to make a scene. I only liked scenes on television. But Lord, could my mama be a star with how many she'd created.

"Okay. Total two hundred and forty-six dollars please. Thank you." He hit a few buttons on the meter and waited for Mama to hand a card up.

"Pull into a spot for me, real quick," Mama said, digging through her purse like she was fishing out her wallet. He turned the steering wheel seamlessly left and we slid straight into a parking spot up front. Mama sighed and gave a weary smile. "Can I share my testimony with you?"

"Please. Please. Two-forty-six, miss."

"Call me Sallie; we rode this long," Mama said, humanizing herself like this was a hostage situation.

"Two-forty-six, Sallie, two-forty-six. We talk long enough." He wasn't even looking at her through the rearview mirror anymore. He had a karate chop hand in the air to show directness and the other gripping the wheel tight. Mama started telling him how she was a single mother, raising two girls on her own, and how she had a brain tumor when I was born. I let my mind wander out of the car, out of the parking lot, out of the city, all the way back to my sister, alone with her garbage bag of clothes. I'd miss her Scooby-Doo sleep shirts and Sailor Moon stickered journals, and having someone to live all this with me.

I'd heard Mama's testimony a thousand times. Old Testament and New. **Book of Sallie Carol 2:3: If you don't have money, give your testimony.** It invites the listener to become part of a blessing. She preached it mostly to landlords and bill collectors. People who could be swayed by the grace of God to help us survive. Yet our cabbie kept his eyes trained out the window, blank faced while Mama talked herself blue. After five full minutes of testifying, she finally reached her point.

"I'm just asking you to let us go. If you could just let us go." She whispered it, like he might lock the doors and speed us toward a police station any second.

The man shook his head before smacking the steering wheel as hard as he could. "Waste my time!" We heard the doors unlock and he hit the steering wheel again. "Get the fuck out! Go!"

We leaped out fast while he continued to pound his steering wheel, cursing in another language. He sped forward from the parking spot, fast enough for us to hear his tires screeching as he peeled off.

Mama looked down at me and nodded. "By the grace of God." **Book of Sallie Carol 6:6: If you've got nothing else, have faith.** Mama's was unyielding. She ascertained every win to the most on high. I gave the glory to her.

She rubbed my shoulders momentarily before leading me toward the automatic doors. "Come on, let's walk around in here a bit." Mama let me play in the books and toy sections while she pressed her cell phone to her ear, no doubt searching for help.

We pretended to shop at first. Walking slow as hell through the towel aisle, bathroom accessories, lamps. It wasn't stimulating at all, because we had just been there earlier with Samantha. My feet were getting tired, but we had to play normal, pushing our book bags around in a cart. We window-shopped until midnight. Mama gave me a nod toward the in-store Subway, and we waited while the workers finished counting the register, wiping the counters, and cutting the lights. It felt like we were casing the joint, but we just needed a booth. A place to slide into for the night.

A security guard walked past us, eyed Mama. She started digging in her purse, pulled out her phone and an address book, started flipping through it like we were busy. The guard kept walking, but he looked back at us, mumbled something into his walkie-talkie. This could go south quick.

The security guard walked past us again, lips pursed but his eyes trained forward.

"I'ma figure something out, baby," Mama crooned to me like a lullaby. From what I could gather, she had done all her figuring for my sister. I tried to lean back in the booth a little. Rest my eyes. But there was never time for rest.

"Evening, ma'am." A legitimate police officer saddled up to our booth in the darkened Walmart Subway. A white man with thin pink lips. The black security guard who had eyed us stood behind the officer with his hand on his belt like he had done something. *Just raggedy.* The cop cleared his throat. "It's awful late to have a child out, isn't it?"

How the hell were we getting out of this one? I could not be separated from Mama. That was the whole thing. Staying together. I searched my database of watching Mama for what I could do. That's how *I* figured things out. I observed everything, staying as informed as a child could be in grown folks' business.

Crying for the police officer was an option, but it might make things worse. Instead, I concentrated on looking nourished and innocent.

The Subway booth had become a vehicle we were trapped in. Mama handed him her license, with her smiling pretty in red lipstick in the photo, and he walked back over to his security guard buddy to check it out.

Mama didn't say anything to me, and I didn't say anything to her. I learned quickly how annoying little-kid questions can be. Sometimes we want a truth that parents can't give us. Either they don't know enough or they know too much, and I never wanted to hurt Mama's feelings with a question. She kept looking at her black book of contacts, so I closed my eyes and laid my head back. Clocking out for the both of us. Maybe she was coming up with a plan.

What if the cop came back asking if we knew anything about a stiffed cabdriver? Mama would have to tell her testimony again. The officer sidled back over real smooth.

"I, um. The system's showing a warrant out for your arrest, ma'am." He sounded almost apologetic.

"What?" Mama's eyes got big. Had the cabdriver really put a hit out on us over a couple hours of driving?

"It says you wrote a bad check in Charlotte, North Carolina, ma'am. I'm going to have to take you in." No emotion showed in his eyes. The Walmart security guard looked smug in the background, happy he had followed his instincts and caught a big fish—a Warranted Woman with a Wee Little Girl! Really keeping the aisles clean.

He didn't handcuff Mama. I think he felt my eyes watching his every move. I could make myself invisible or hyper-visible if the situation called for the reminder of a child's presence. I wanted him to really feel a baby in the room, a mommy in custody. He made us walk in front of him all the way out of the store, then opened the door of his police car and went tight-lipped, ushering Mama and me to see ourselves in.

I hated when I didn't have the full story, and I rarely did as an eight-year-old. Mama gave me enough of the uncensored truth for me to understand what was going on, but that only made me crave more truth from the rest of the world.

From what I could make of it later, Mama needed a car real bad after my daddy took off with his white woman. She wanted a new city, and she needed a way to get there, so she went to the car dealership. A brand-new 1991 Buick caught her attention. She could picture her whole future in that car. Riding it all the way to Atlanta to start her own business. So she took a leap of faith using one of her tried-and-true methods. ***Book of Sallie Carol 2:5: Check now, cash later.*** Checks don't get cashed right away, so you have time to put money in the bank to cover things like food or school clothes. Especially if you write it on a Friday and let the weekend stretch the time.

She wrote a check for several thousand dollars in that car dealership. A check attached to an account with something like eight hundred dollars in it, which she would withdraw before the check cleared. Mama figured she'd be moving into a new apartment in another state, miles away, by the time the check bounced. She wasn't *stealing* a car. She said she planned to pay it back, she just needed time to make the money. Two years later, she gave the car to a couple in need, free of charge. I'm not sure if it was virtuous or her getting rid of it.

None of this was revealed to me in the back of that police car. We were both arrested. She in one way, me in another. Hours passed as I sat on a police bench at the station waiting for something to happen.

My aunt drove all the way from North Carolina to Georgia to get me. Mama told Aunt Mattie to keep me safe, and then the two of us traveled back to Greensboro. I fell asleep along the dark stretch of trees and highway and woke up in another reality.

The scriptures from Mama's book didn't quite apply at Aunt Mattie's house. I could sense something was already going on with Auntie, her own personal struggles. Too many loud whispers behind closed doors. The daughter from her first love, Cousin Latrice, was a little older than Samantha and headed back to college, which was fine by me, because the looks she threw my way implied she thought I was trying to replace her. In reality, I was grateful to sleep in her bed. Cousin Ronnie Jr. was a year older than me, and sweet as candy but with emerging developmental challenges. Meanwhile, my uncle Ronnie Sr. started appearing at fewer and fewer dinners. Aunt Mattie had the same brave face as Mama, except she wouldn't tell me what was behind it like Mama did.

Book of Sallie Carol 3:1: Education is key. Knowledge drives you forward. Thus, life with Aunt Mattie became about attaining information. And for a kid like me, observation was free schooling. I mostly wanted intel pertaining to me or to Mama, but such tidbits were few and far between. I needed to know if she was okay, if my sister was okay, and if I would be staying permanently.

Of the shelves full of movies at Aunt Mattie's, *Harriet the Spy* was my favorite. She knew the only way to get information as a kid was to steal it. I modeled my life after hers for a full month. I kept a notepad tucked in my back pocket and listened to every phone call Aunt Mattie received, pressing against the back of the couch in the den to eavesdrop. It was creepy, writing down gossip on her coworkers and sisters from the church, and also one-sided. The juiciest parts were probably whispered in her ear, and I wasn't bold enough to grab the other phone and listen in.

Against my will, I was enrolled in the elementary school across the street with Junior. It felt too permanent. I much preferred the idea of Cinderellaing in Auntie's guest room, hiding away from the world until I could go home. The summer had been fun. Each day, I made Junior learn extensive plays that I had written, not on paper, but out loud as we improvised. The millisecond Aunt Mattie got home from work, we'd rush her to the couch in the den and make her watch our performance. I loved our Peter Pan and Wendy days: running from wasps when we explored too far from the house, making up games in the big grassed backyard. I loved just playing.

Now I was forced at a moment's notice to socialize with people I might never see again. It was fine. Nothing I wasn't used to. Back home I'd attended two different elementary schools because of our evictions.

Schoolwork was like memorizing lines to me. There was valuable information and disposable information. Things like the red cardinal being the state bird of North Carolina I only had to remember long enough to pass a test.

Now that I didn't have to hide living in a dingy hotel, I could develop friendships instead of avoiding them and their questions. I had two best friends in Greensboro, Brooke and Nicole. I still didn't want to delve into my home life too much. But in the country, no one really questioned if you lived with your auntie or your grandma. That's just how things were for some folks. Brooke had big curly hair and Nicole was white. Being best friends meant playing on the jungle gym, eating lunch together, and sharing secrets on the phone.

This was major to me. For one, I had a house phone normal kids could call. I wouldn't have to give them the number for a motel and have them ask the front desk lady for our room number. Aunt Mattie even had two house phones! One in the living room and one in her bedroom. I knew a ringing phone was for me when she faked a frown and put her hand on her hip. "Someone's giggling for you, little girl," she'd say, and hand me the cordless. I'd run smiling to the den, hunkering down on the couch while my cousin played Nintendo. He was happy not to pass me the controller for a turn when Mario died underwater.

Once Nicole asked me if I liked Brooke's clothes and I said, "I guess so," because I spent too many years worrying about my own ensembles to talk bad about someone else's. And wouldn't you know it, Brooke came giggling out of the darkness of the phone, announcing we were in a *three-way call* and I didn't know. My heart raced with relief at not having said anything bad, but then I got mad. Mama was right. *People play games.* I'd almost make it scripture, but you can't let these people know you're on to them. You can't trust anybody.

After the girls put me on to the three-way trap, I feared Aunt

Mattie or the jail security guards were listening to my phone calls with Mama, and that our conversations needed to be coded. Mama mostly told me she loved me, God would get us through, and that she'd see me soon. She'd whisper for me to look out for her letters. Written correspondence was private—at least after Aunt Mattie and the jail security read it.

Mama sometimes referred to things from letters I didn't receive. On phone calls with Samantha in her college dorm, I whispered that I wasn't sure Auntie gave me all my mail. So my sister wrote me a letter every day for at least two weeks, each envelope handmade from magazine pages—Lip Smacker ads and Delia's teen fashion models—the address written on a white square glued to the outside, inscribed in her tiny handwriting. That way there would be so many letters Auntie couldn't hold them. Samantha flooded me with love via colorful envelopes, and I grinned so big when Auntie handed them to me.

My sister wrote energetically about classes and dorm food and anime and boys. I would giggle in the corner of the bed, smelling each letter, counting them anew every time one arrived, until the day Auntie handed me a white envelope. I recognized Mama's bold, loopy handwriting immediately. Auntie had already opened it and stood in the doorway watching while I pawed the letter out from between the tear marks.

Years later, Aunt Mattie admitted that she did withhold some of Mama's letters. She said they had too much information inside. Things an eight-year-old shouldn't know, shouldn't have to deal with. It struck me that she was right. But back then, I was starved for the truth and finally being fed when I got this letter. I thought again of the difference between disposable and vital information.

If I'm allowed to know something at eight years old, that means it's vital, which terrified me.

Mommy has to tell you something. Don't be scared. We have to have faith in God. The doctors say Mommy has breast cancer. I have to take chemotherapy to heal. And it will make all my hair fall out like Mr. Clean. But Mommy will be okay.

She'd drawn a little picture of Mr. Clean on the side. Grinning with a bald head. My teachers said I read at an accelerated level. That I could comprehend things. I did not want to comprehend this.

What was I supposed to do with this information? My future self would remember this moment. I wasn't just some little girl. I understood what Mama wrote whether she drew a picture or not. I was scared, but I was brave. And I had faith in Mama. If she said she was gonna be all right, she would be all right.

After I spent almost a full year with Aunt Mattie, Mama came to get me. Tension hovered in the air between the sisters. Mama had taken a bus from Atlanta to Greensboro after she was released from jail and got settled. I was eager to know our economic status after her stint in the clink and about the breast cancer. She wasn't immediately forthcoming, just hugged me tight, swayed with my tiny body between her legs and pressed into her stomach while she told her sister about the trip.

I assessed her clothing. Khaki pants, plain white top. We were still wearing staples. Aunt Mattie had me in *Hercules* and *Rugrats* T-shirts, so I was alienated from Mama in that respect.

It was spaghetti night. Mama spoke cordial at the table. I felt weird being witnessed this normal, like I lived in the house and Mama lived outside it. I wanted Mama and me to have an inside, but I also didn't mind being on the outside with her. After Junior and I had slurped up our noodles and eaten a little pound cake for dessert, Mama asked me to join her in the living room to talk and pray. I stood to follow her. Aunt Mattie told me to go bathe and get ready for bed since there was school tomorrow. My body froze in place between the kitchen and the hallway to the living room. Who did I take commands from? Mama or the hand that feeds me?

I started to cry. Mama fussed at Aunt Mattie while her hands pushed me toward the bathroom. That night, Mama shared the guest room bed with me. She prayed over my head at full volume, never one to shy away from others knowing about her relationship with God or hearing the level of pleas she had to make to keep us covered in the blood of Jesus. After she prayed, she whispered to me in the dark for a while. She wasn't going to let Aunt Mattie keep me. She was my mother. I lay still, feigning sleep until it came.

I woke to a scuffle, right on top of me. When my eyes fluttered open in the dark room, I was witnessing something biblical. White silk nightgowns shifting smooth in a rough battle. A fight between sisters, two angels watching over one baby, both thinking the other Lucifer. And who would fall from grace?

My mother's hands punched at her little sister, and she swatted back. My uncle Ronnie burst in and pulled them apart. Mama would leave on a Greyhound bus back to Georgia the next day, and I would take an airplane alone a couple months later.

The flight attendant called me sweetheart when she asked what snack I wanted. She walked me all the way off the plane after landing and didn't leave my side until Mama came waving toward me. These things made me feel special. Cared for.

Mama's hair was bone straight instead of a curly Afro. Something new. If her hair was different, our whole lives could be too. Maybe this was her stable-life hair. We took the train from the airport and rode it into the city for about forty-five minutes; then Mama held my hand while we boarded a bus.

The anticipation sent shock waves of anxiety through my lanky-legged body. Mama wasn't telling me everything. Were we about to pull up to an affordable flat-level home or a nice enough apartment complex? How settled had Mama gotten before she reclaimed me? How normal would we get to be? We rode by the county jail, and I held my breath like we were passing a graveyard. Was that where Mama had been? She didn't turn her head to look out the window.

For the entire bus ride, she did that thing where she talked fast and energetically about every topic in the world except the one you cared about. "Miss Shirley sued her job after the work injury. She getting a big ole payout and won't have to work for months. Burger King claimed they were hiring, but when they saw my degrees they turned me down. You can't win for losing."

Mama absentmindedly pulled the cord to alert the driver we needed to get off. The bus slowed and came to a stop along Memorial Drive. My heart started racing. There weren't any houses on this street and the apartments were farther down. She took my hand in hers and we exited our ride. This was where we were in life. Memorial Drive Inn hotel. My stomach sloshed with bile, but I gave Mama a reassuring smile. In my head, I figured if this was hard for me, it was probably hard for her to do it to me. We walked forward toward our street-facing room on the second floor.

Mama waved hello to a family with their hotel room door

propped open like there was a porch to let in a breeze. I saw two kids younger than me playing with dolls on a full-size bed, and their mama talking on the room phone from the other bed. Mama held my hand tighter while we squeezed past two men in wifebeaters leaning over the rail talking. Then she tapped a plastic card against the third door down, the green light flashed, and we were inside. It was the same setup as the family I'd just seen had, although Samantha would be home soon from precollege, so two beds meant we were sharing. "You've got your sleeping bag now too," Mama said, referring to the *Rugrats* bag Aunt Mattie got me for Christmas that was now stuffed into my book bag. "You can camp out in front of the TV if you want." I nodded, almost overly agreeable, convincing myself and Mama that this was all okay. We were together. We were together. We were together. Most important part.

Mama turned the television on to a movie playing on TBS for some background noise. Maybe *Twister*. She went to the bathroom to freshen up and then came out looking at me with a thin-lipped grin. "You wanna see how Mommy is different now? Since the cancer?" This scared me, but I didn't want her to leave me out of knowing again. I needed to be prepared at all times for walking into a hotel or a sickness. This anxiety was unacceptable. I shouldn't have expected so much to be different. She was offering to show me now. I nodded, wide-eyed.

"Mommy wears a wig now. This is a wig." Her unusually straight short hair slid right off at her soft tug and rested in her hand like a pet hamster. She stood before me bald and smiling bright. What else could I do but keep nodding? Under no circumstance would I hurt her feelings with a tear-jerk reaction. This was her story. I was her witness.

"You still look good, Mama," I told her.

"Now," she said. "Do you want to see my new breast?" Things were escalating quickly. She lifted up her shirt. "Don't get skittish on me. It's all right. It doesn't hurt." Mama got bras from T.J. Maxx, and she firmly believed that the number and letter sizing were all made-up gibberish. She said grab whatever looks like it fits, so her bras rarely had that round, pointy shape to them, but they weren't bad. She lifted her ill-fitted white lacy bra, and I noted that one side was more ill fitted than the other. Her right breast came out like normal, answering gravity, full and brown. The other was stiff. Something new. Sculpted. It still looked like brown flesh, but artificially formed. A breast that didn't hang. And what's more, there was no nipple. Just stitches that formed an areola shape, with nothing inside it. I stared.

"Mommy's nipple fell off." The words weren't processing for me. Mama touched her new breast like it was no big deal. "The doctors said don't remove the bandages for a week, but I got too anxious to see." She rubbed with her finger where a nipple should be. "It hadn't healed enough, fell right off." My eyebrows raised. My mother stood before me, bald and one-breasted and real. I was thankful to know and to see. I took a step toward her and reached. She smiled, grabbing my hand and placing it right in the middle of her areola stitches. I tried not to flinch. This was Mama's body. *Take, eat,* my Christian brain added. Mama put her breasts back inside her bra and pulled her shirt down. She left her wig off, saying it can get hot and itchy after a while and that her real hair should grow back soon.

We lay together on the hotel bed, snacking on a ninety-nine-cent bag of Cheetos. What I didn't focus on during my last months at Aunt Mattie's were Mama's doctors' appointments and trips. She had a few while in jail. That's how she got her diagnosis. And then after she got out, there was the surgery—the doctors needed to remove her left breast before the cancer spread. So with Samantha in West Georgia and the rest of Mama's family in North Carolina, she did the twelve-hour procedure alone.

After the surgery, she thought she'd be able to rest at Grady Memorial Hospital for a week or so, but then within a few hours they asked her who was picking her up. "No one," she said. "I don't have anyone in town with me." And without even a blink of sympathy they said they needed the bed for the next person. With her body aching, chest freshly cut and sewn, they plopped her into a wheelchair and pushed her out to the curb. She told me all this while *Twister* played soft in the background.

The mental picture made my stomach hurt with sorrow. I hugged Mama's middle real tight. She squeezed me back. The movie went to commercial break. "They left me out there alone. But your mama is strong. I did what I do. Used a child support check to get this room. We gon' be all right. Mama's healing."

This level of information was best paired with Mama's unwavering faith. It made things manageable, survivable. The movie came back on. We snuggled our bodies together, eyes trained forward.

September

It's the end of September now. Everything feels normal. Maybe things will be like before. Maybe Mama will live. At family reunions, her siblings joke that she'll outlast everyone. If she can get a stable place, if she can get back on her feet and start working again, maybe she'll be okay.

You lie in bed watching *The X-Files* on DVDs your sister got you for your birthday. The phone buzzes in your hand. Mama. It's the type of day where you don't hesitate to answer.

She's in a good mood. You can tell because she says, "Hey, Poo," in that cheerful voice she only uses when she isn't worried about money. Or where she will go. Or how she will eat. It's her healthy voice. You say, "Hi, Mama," and ask where she is. The background is silent. Unsettlingly so.

"They put me up in a nice place."

What does that mean? You ask her what nice place they have put her in, and who "they" are. Your mother uses this pronoun often. "They." And it's important to establish who "they" are before she gets lost in conversation and her own trail of thoughts.

"I was at the hospital and they asked if I had anywhere to go.

I told them no. And they arranged for me to have a nice place to stay."

You ask your mother what she means. In your experience, in *her* experience, the hospitals were not so kind.

"It's beautiful here. I'm down the street from the baseball stadium. You know? Like the Atlanta Braves. And I can see a beautiful forest outside. It's very tucked away. And I stay in a nice room. It's all mine. I have a bed and a television. There aren't many channels. I don't think it's cable, but you know, I would rather just sit and read my Bible. There's a nice bedside stand in here for me.... Everyone is really nice. There's like a living room area for us to sit in and watch movies and stuff. It's nice."

You are afraid but don't know why. It's about the money, you tell yourself. You can't afford to pay for anything and are unsure if any of your aunts and uncles will help. You ask her how much this is costing.

"It doesn't cost me anything. My doctors told me, 'Sallie, you don't have to worry about anything,'" she says in one of her silly voices. "They told me I ain't have to pay for *NOTHING*. It's all covered in my insurance. I probably won't stay too long. Just until I can get situated again. I need to focus on my work. I realize now what my dream is. I want to open my own school. Freedom Peace never quite caught on, but I can make it into more than just counseling. It can be—"

"Where are you?" You don't like to cut her off, but she rambles. She can carry a conversation for hours by herself if no one stops her. So you ask where exactly she is before she changes the subject. She is cunning.

"It's called Halcyon Hospice. A very nice place."

She said the name in an awkward voice. As if she was getting used to it herself. As if she has heard one definition but understands another. You put her on speakerphone and google the word "hospice," envisioning a hospital. The results show places that look like nursing homes. You click on a link for Halcyon Hospice, Atlanta. You had googled "Halcion." You read the caption: "Our mission is to comfort patients and families struggling with a serious illness. Halcyon Hospice is committed to delivering the highest quality end-of-life care with dignity, compassion and love."

Something in your inner ear shatters. Something in your stomach expands. Something in your heart tears. Something in your brain leaks hot flicks of electricity. You say something out loud to your mother, but you're not sure what.

"Don't worry about anything, Poo. All this is temporary. I'm using this place to get back on my feet. I'm not staying here longer than a week or so. These doctors have no say over my God, you hear me? You understand what I'm saying? You there?"

Everything is broken now. You are miles away, physically and mentally. Drifting toward 1998. Your mother is honest, even if her goals of getting out don't match the hospice tagline. She wants you to believe *her*, not the doctors. She needs you to believe she will survive. Something inside you screams the truth. Your mother is receiving the highest-quality end-of-life care.

North

Mama did it wrong, the Great Migration. She went deeper south, instead of north, burying us in a black mecca of dreamers and schemers where freedom was still out of reach. Poverty was consuming us like quicksand. When even the hotel rooms became too expensive to maintain, the three of us moved in with a lady from church, uncomfortably sharing a bedroom in her house while she complained we were running up her light bill. The way I saw it, Samantha and I would be the Simpson family's final tries at liberation.

Mama was trying to keep us afloat with her counseling business between teaching jobs. She kept in contact with Henry, the speaker who'd inspired her big move to Atlanta, often talking on the phone excitedly behind her bedroom door. He'd solved a string of children's murders in the eighties. He'd been on the news! He would speak for free at the small conferences she was able to pull together through Freedom Peace. The five or six women who showed up got a local celebrity guest speaker and Mama got paid.

Mama told us his latest ex-wife hated that she and Henry were close, that she didn't like him working with a younger woman. They only got closer. Henry tried building a relationship with Samantha and me as well. He would roll up in a big black SUV that had his name in all capital letters on the license plate, steering wheel pressed against his belly. He took us to places that served *good* southern food, called me baby girl, complimented Samantha's brilliance, and listened to Mama's stories about her backstabbing coworkers, then paid for everything with crisp twenties. The people running the restaurant always knew who Henry was, always sat us at nice tables.

His all-encompassing success and captivating know-how made him Mama's kind of man. He was the personification of ***Book of Sallie Carol 3:1: Education is key. Knowledge drives you forward*** and in all forms: books, streets, people. Proof that Mama's efforts could pay off. You have to know something to do something.

Things took a tentative turn for the better once Mama landed a job teaching middle school science. We lived in a decent apartment with an upstairs and downstairs for the last half of my middle school years. I had best friends again, Shani and Zavieta, and relished weekend sleepovers, thirteenth-birthday parties, and even a Scream Tour concert featuring Lil' Bow Wow and B2K.

Samantha was up at Kenyon College in Ohio now, working on her dream of becoming a fiction writer. She'd certainly made it her aesthetic, with daily journaling in notebooks she decorated, stacks of library books, and colorful highlighted school notes. She was smart as hell. Made enough As to earn scholarship money and have her pick of where she wanted to escape. Meanwhile, I'd spent the school year flunking ninth-grade math and was now forced to face the consequences.

Mama had already booked a two-week educator's course in Boston and was not changing her plans, so it would be up to Samantha, home from college, to get me to and from summer school. She hated this. In her mind, she was Alicia Keys in the "You Don't Know My Name" music video, working at the tea shop in the mall while eyeing her crush from the camera store across the way, not a babysitter.

Mama insisted on having her moment. She pulled out her usual scripture, **Stay close to your sister. You'll be all each other has one day (1:9)**, blatantly hinting at her inevitable death. Forcing us to prepare for a bleak future when in the present she was headed up north, off to enjoy her version of freedom.

My godmother, Miss Joyce, who pulled me from between Mama's legs when I was born, called from Florida to add extra incentive—she'd give me a check for one hundred dollars if I passed the math course with an A. I worked hard for the money, if nothing else.

Summer school made me anxious. It felt like the academy for villains and class clowns, too many antagonists. The whole environment felt seedy. This was my first lesson on what happens when you don't apply yourself—you end up in the underbelly. I befriended a girl named Jameelah, another regular person, and we spent breaks writing *Angel* fan fiction in a shared notebook to get through the days.

Samantha would pick me up and make me sit in the tea shop during her shift. I wasn't even allowed to wander the mall. It made me pissy, taking orders from my sister instead of movie recommendations and jokes. I passed the time reading Lurlene McDaniel novels about kids with cancer, titled things like *Too Young to Die*.

The night before my fifteenth birthday, Samantha and I got into our only physical altercation. I was mad at her because she wouldn't let me stay home alone while she worked. We ended up tussling all over the living room carpet. She grabbed the house phone and started hitting me upside the head while I shielded myself until I screamed that I'd listen to her. An hour later it was more humorous than traumatic, but we still maintained our silence until bedtime.

In the morning, my sister made no acknowledgment of my birthday. Not a word over cold cereal nor when she dropped me off at summer school. I tried to match her energy, even as it made me sad. I decided to sound pathetic on the phone if Mama called from Boston.

When Samantha pulled up to get me, her face was stone cold, but she had a silly hat on. "Get in," she said, handing me a party hat shaped like a British crown with *I Rule* embroidered on the front. I put it on and we rode back home in silence.

When she opened the door to our apartment, everything was decorated: a banner, balloons, confetti, and a cake right in the middle of the living room table. "Happy Birthday!" she exclaimed, showing emotion for the first time all day. My heart swelled and my cheeks hurt from smiling, and I understood what Mama meant about sisters.

When I was born, Mama and Samantha were hurting from the loss of a husband and father, each coping in her own way. Mama says when I was just a few weeks old, Samantha, almost eight, removed the pictures from the walls and poured flour all over me in the crib. I have a clear memory from age three of simply waiting outside a door my sister had closed in my face. Yet she was the coolest person in the world to me. As a teenager, Samantha wore dark blue nail polish with silver glitter cuz Mama said no black. She watched *Sailor Moon* and *Ranma ½* and I did too because she did. When I was thirteen, she finally said I was funny and we got to be good friends, able to communicate in quick glances when Mama did something off-kilter.

Samantha and I rode around town all that summer in the Ford Focus Mama helped her get. Hitting up Media Play for DVDs and books that she'd buy me with her tea shop paychecks, then having lunch at the Cici's Pizza or the Chinese Buffet 2000 on Memorial Drive. Best friends. I'd tape *Buffy the Vampire Slayer* on VHS when she went on dates with her boyfriend. Mad she missed it, but excited to ask her what dating was like. It was a relief, having a sister, someone who comes from where you're from, bears witness during your childhood, survives what you survived.

I passed math that summer with a straight-up 100 and got just as many dollars from my godmother, Miss Joyce, as promised. Mama made it back from Boston in one piece, more educated and confident and ready to get her business off the ground than ever. It was the best summer. When Samantha came home for her twenty-third in October, I pulled the birthday hat back out and made her wear it to a fancy Chinese spot. It became our tradition: the hat, being together.

One night, Mama decided to take Samantha's car instead of her Buick and, enlisting me as an accomplice, drove us to Chinese Buffet 2000 for dinner while Samantha was out with a friend. Mama justified that Samantha wouldn't have the car if she hadn't helped her get it, so she was perfectly allowed to take it for a spin if she wanted. I said nothing, staring out the window as Mama drove us to the restaurant.

We ate; we drove back. When we opened the front door, Samantha was standing there fuming, waiting for us to enter.

"Where were you!" she yelled.

Mama pinched her lips together, putting her purse down like she was in no rush and nothing was wrong. "We went and grabbed a bite at the Chinese place." She spoke evenly, refusing to match Samantha's tone.

"Why did you take my car?"

"Why not?"

"I thought somebody stole it! You can't just take things without asking."

"You wouldn't *have* that car if it wasn't for me, missy. I can take—"

"It's mine. That's the whole point!"

"*It's mines. It's mines,*" Mama said in a mocking voice. "Just like when you was little, grabbing toys—"

"I'm grown, Mama!"

They went back and forth in the living room. Even though we were within three inches of each other in height, it felt like they were a million feet above me.

Mama went upstairs and Samantha followed, both screaming at the top of their lungs. My heart raced. Mama rushed into Samantha's room at the top of the stairs, grabbing CDs, books, and VHS tapes to toss around while she asserted herself as the boss.

"Calm down! Please!" I shouted, terrified at this escalation. "Mama, stop!" But my volume felt muted by their fight. Samantha grabbed for her things from Mama's hands, and Mama pushed her away with one arm. Rage flashed across Samantha's face like I'd never seen before, and she shoved Mama back.

"Samantha! Stop!"

Mama huffed like a bull about to charge and the two of them lunged at each other, slapping, squeezing middles, shoving, and coming back together. Their bodies wrestled toward the door and a horrible image of them tumbling down the stairs and breaking their necks haunted my mind's eye. I screamed and shouted, tears running down my face, and threw my body in front of the stairs, blocking it with my arms. Like a tornado changing course, their bodies swayed back inside the bedroom, and they fell onto Samantha's bed, finally tearing away from each other as they bounced.

"*Get out!*" Mama screamed, jumping to her feet and adjusting her top. "Pack your shit and get the hell out of my house. You can live in the damn car for all I care." She went to her room and slammed the door.

Samantha jumped up, yanked her shirts from the closet like in a movie scene, and started packing.

I cried while she placed her journals and flannel button-downs and sleep shirts into her book bag. She kept her face emotionless. I trailed behind her and her roller suitcase all the way downstairs and out to the parking lot, following her like I did when I was three. Her car sat perfectly spotlighted under the glow of a streetlamp. After she loaded her things into the backseat beside her white teddy bear, Stanley, she turned to me with tears on her cheeks. We hugged each other tight.

"I don't want you to go," I mumbled into her chest.

"I'll call you, okay. And I'll write you letters." The thought

of receiving letters from her like 1998 made fresh tears gurgle up
and she pulled me away to stare hard into my eyes. "We're sisters,
always."

We swayed under the streetlamp for another minute before
saying, "I love you." We were *The Color Purple*, pulling away from
each other backward. I watched her drive out of the apartment
complex and down Covington Highway, before turning to go
inside.

Mama was waiting for me at the door, brow furrowed. "You
got something to say? Cuz if so, you can leave right with her."

My gaze sank to the floor. "No."

A week or so went by. Samantha and I became talk-on-the-
phone-every-day sisters. She was staying in the attic room at
her friend's house, writing in her journals dramatically about
what had happened and watching *Fushigi Yûgi* on VHS. Mama
pretended she didn't care where her elder baby was by keeping
busy with her work. I tried to stay loyal to both sides. Dropping
only the tiniest bits of information between the two of them:
Samantha's safe. / Mama's working.

Aunt Vernell, the second oldest, called Mama to recite a verse
from her own book of advice: "Never throw away your babies."
Having them, raising them, watching them grow into themselves
and the world, is a blessing. So Mama went and got Samantha.

That's why you have to be close to your sister. They keep your
head on straight. Gather you when you need gathering.

Samantha came back. Mama drove her own car. They were
cordial if not a little icy, though Samantha and I were closer than
ever. I think Mama liked that. The corner of her mouth drew up
in a smile as she listened to Samantha and me cackling in the

living room while she wrote in her notebooks. We'd be fine with or without her. I think she liked that a lot.

By the time I was in tenth grade, we were renting a house in the type of neighborhood where people go all out with Christmas lights for the holidays. Our place was smaller than the ones up front, but we still got to drive through TV-esque residentials to get to our driveway. Fifteen-year-old me had it easier than any other version of myself, which could be good or bad in a karmic sense. Four years of relative stability promised something dark ahead.

In the middle of my junior year, Mama called me into her room, sat me on the edge of the bed, and pulled a pamphlet from her bedside table. A trifold, just like her business brochures. The one she held was titled *What to Do Next* and decorated with pink ribbons. Beneath the title, bald women smiled wide and clutched onto each other. She spoke gently.

"The cancer is back." She paused, allowing me time to process. I wasn't sure what to say. It was happening again. The recurring nightmare we were trapped inside. Sickness startling us awake every time we dared to rest.

"They say I could live up to five more years. But I know my God, and I think I have a lot more time left in me." Mama winked. Like the cancer was in the room with us and we were sharing an inside joke.

I tried to comprehend. "Do you have to take chemo again?" My eyes were trained on the happy bald women in the pamphlet. Mrs. Cleans. I wondered if they were still alive.

"I'm going to avoid it as long as possible. So Mommy doesn't get weak. You know I got big goals for my business."

Five years. She'd beaten it before. Was she strong enough to do it again? Maybe it was more about accomplishing her goals while she was still here. I could already tell from her tone that she was going to use everything she had—not to heal, but to hustle.

Which meant I had to do the same. I needed to become somebody before time ran out. What if the only way forward was on me? How could I give both of us a future?

A perk of being the baby girl was that I could learn from both Mama and Samantha, take what worked and leave the rest. Samantha had ridden **Verse 3:1** on education all the way up north. I respected it, but it wasn't my style. Education was too slow and steady wins the race for me; I needed big coin if I was gonna save me and Mama from the clutches of check-to-check living. Mama had a plethora of licenses and degrees and it hadn't protected us from anything. But I'd had something simmering for a while now.

Family lore said that when I was only a few months old Grandma Jamie dreamed she saw me on television, her grand-baby performing for an audience. Too bad she didn't see anything about her son not raising me, but she dropped a prophecy at least. My audition for local television in fourth grade may not have gone anywhere, but the dream never left my veins.

There was a year and a half left of high school, five alleged years left of Mama. Logically speaking, I needed to get to Holly-wood. I just had to focus on the vision. If life was a stage, whatever was supposed to happen could start right here in the classroom.

In Decatur, Georgia, high school swayed like Motown. Judg-ing from the old bullet hole lodged in one of the front windows of Towers, you'd think our boys were gang-banging, but really they were rapping. Any one of them could be the next Fabo, T.I.,

Lil Jon & the East Side Boyz. At lunch you'd hear fists beating against tabletops, a mouth *tititing*, and then somebody would start freestyling about being fresh to death and running the city. Soulja Boy was our age and he had popped from cranking his dance all over YouTube. A couple guys from our school got a hit on the radio called "Juke Ya Boi." It seemed like the only way to make it onward and upward was entertainment.

Not to be outdone, the girls were singing soulful in the bathroom stalls between classes. Their crew would whoop and shout and encourage each other to audition for *American Idol*. A girl from Towers made it past the first round but then got cut, though you'd have sworn she had an album out from our reaction.

In tenth grade, I'd formed a clique: Me, Amber, Courtney, Krystal, and Uche. We came to call ourselves Le Entourage and hung tight in all our AP classes, laughing nonstop. A girl sat in one of our unofficial assigned seats once and we got so irritated that we wrote a diss track. Rapping her name backward and calling her a ho, we realized we had potential, and made Le Entourage a rap group.

We performed our debut track, "Eat Me Out," in the gymnasium and during our lunch period. Both times, we were met with jeers from the boys, who only wanted to hear other boys rap about getting their dicks sucked. Not to be discouraged, Krystal and I used the studio in her basement at home. The girls from Crime Mob had recorded a track with her stepfather in the same room!

It took us a whole Saturday afternoon to get it perfect. When we played it for her mother, stepfather, and sisters that night, we smiled with anticipation, praying they'd say we had what it took to make the radio, become local legends, get signed, and end up holding microphones on *106 & Park* with Free and AJ. Instead, they balked at our fifteen-year-old asses begging for head on the track and her mother yanked the CD from the boombox and snapped it in half.

Rap had been a detour. Girl groups weren't the way. Beyoncé had just left Destiny's Child after all. It was time for me to break out. Sports was an option, but it worked better for the football boys. My friend Ellen had already been the girl who played football on the boys' team, so that niche was taken. Volleyball had cute uniforms, but I was only good at serving. I tried my hand at soccer, playing some decent defense, but I wasn't full-ride-to-college good at all. I tore my ACL before the season was out.

Inspired by my pages of fan fiction, I gave writing a try, circulating a novella I'd handwritten in a spiral notebook titled *Zane* with a picture of the rapper Zane glued on top and starring a character named Zane, who was supersmart and trying to get out of the ghetto but gets shot and killed before he can make it. Riveting stuff, but after a few passes around school I wasn't sure what to do next.

I wanted to occupy a space that no one had been inside. Drama class presented itself as an entry point to Hollywood in my eyes. None of the teenagers around me were interested in being scrutinized onstage, so there was plenty of space for me to shine. I enrolled. It was mostly taken as a sleeper course, taught by a round man named Mr. Sherow who would whack a playbook against the desk when he caught people sleeping, then tell them to read a part. Some of these kids stumbled over every word when they were called on, but I loved to read aloud. My classmates leaned forward as I brought characters to life, making clear the world of the play as I read it. When my paragraph of text was done, my cheeks would blush hot.

I could be the next Oprah! I played her in the skits in class, shouting for my classmates to check under their chairs—"You get detention! You get detention!"—and left them belly laughing. Unlike the other kids in school, I had real motivation. Mama held a ticking clock in her hands, and I was racing against it. With Mr. Sherow's help, I got the abandoned Drama Club reopened and we put on a production of *A Christmas Carol*. I remember nothing about the play except my big scene as Scrooge's girlfriend, getting to wear a dress and act different from myself.

My reputation as the next Raven-Symoné was loading. So far Mama was doing better than she had during the cancer that took her breast. She needed daily pills and personal prayer and her doctors still suggested chemo, but she didn't want it because she needed to work as much as possible. She was teaching DUI now, and the classes were sporadic, which meant sporadic rent payments.

If we didn't answer the phone, the landlord would come in person. We'd see his bald head through the window and still not answer. Sometimes he'd walk through the yard and to the back door, and peer in through the blinds to see if we were home. We would hide upstairs. Mama would call him later and try to work something out. We needed her business to pop now more than ever. We couldn't be poor and sick. That was 1998. A low like that was hard to come back from.

On Saturday afternoons, Mama would type up new outlines for women's conferences on the computer at the desk she set up in our living room while I ate bowls of cereal and watched *The Outer*

Limits on the couch. She'd call me over for emergencies—"Jane, quick! Everything deleted!"—and I would press the undo button; she'd say, "Thank you, Jesus," and click the floppy disk save symbol five or six times before she hit print.

She'd grab her big black purse and a manila folder, and we'd drive over to Office Depot to make copies. I'd sit for an hour or so folding her brochures in three parts and another hour leaving flyers and pamphlets on people's cars or tucked into mailboxes. We hoped this would lead to next month's rent before the bald-headed man put us out. She offered courses, counseling, and conferences at the library, a brilliant mix of self-help, religion, and actual licensed therapy to reel in women from the church and strangers off the street.

This was ingenuity I admired. Even when attendance at the conferences was low, she held them anyway. That's what was important. "You have to do it once to do it twice," she would say.

Mama told me I needed to apply to colleges and handed me a stack of informational three-folds and flip-throughs from institutions across the country. More brochures and pamphlets. I chose some quick ones: UGA, Oswego, and then I zeroed in on a school that boasted Gillian Anderson on the alumni page. Scully from *The X-Files*! That sounded like Hollywood to me. With no further thought, it was decided I wanted this Catholic theater school in Chicago with all of my heart.

I landed an audition for the drama department that was being held in downtown Atlanta. I'd never been to this part of the city before. When Le Entourage was getting wild on the weekend, we rode the train down to Atlantic Station and played in the Target parking lot before window-shopping and going to a movie. That was the big city to me. This was honking cars and tall business buildings, the Fox Theatre standing like a symbol of all I aspired to be, in an environment I could barely keep up with.

Mama, overwhelmed by traffic and irritated with the metered spaces, circled the block endlessly until we found free parking. There were lots of stuffy-looking parents and teens looking either panicked or pinched. I didn't see many black kids. Mama spoke to the lady at the front desk, and I tried to concentrate on my *Raisin in the Sun* monologue. *Me? Me, I'm nothing.* Too on the nose.

There were three full rooms of people auditioning for just fifty spots. And this was one city! What were the chances? Mama led us to sit down in the last open chairs while she filled out a form. I thought about Grandma Jamie's prophecy. Me. On television. I couldn't let statistical realities take me under.

I gave my audition everything I had. We paired off to perform short scenes in different emotions, and that was perfect for me, because I knew you shone brightest in a group with dimmer lights. Three judges evaluated our performances, and one of them was a black lady. I didn't let her eyes go the entire hour I was in that room. I could tell she was feeling me, so I projected all my energy into her and trusted my gut that this Ms. Phyllis would fight for me.

After the scenes, they called us up one by one to do our monologues. When it was my turn, I summoned up a version of myself that commanded the stage. I *was* Beneatha. And I focused on Ms. Phyllis like we were the only ones there.

Two weeks later, I received an eight-by-ten stuffed envelope from the theater school. I held it nervously, but Mama grinned big, already knowing from the size what was inside. "Rip it open, girl!"

Congratulations! the letter proclaimed, covering me in the promise of a brighter future. *We are pleased to inform you . . .*

This was it. My ticket up north. I was following in the family legacy: pursuit. The letter explained that in addition to only selecting fifty-two applicants out of thousands who auditioned, they would only select twenty-six students to continue on in the program after the first year. I could come back home with something concrete or I could end up failing. There was no room to consider any possibility outside of success.

September

Five days a week you clock in and out of your job at the H&M call center. You operate like everything is fine: reciting the script into your headset, searching the system for packages, delivering inconvenient updates to angry voices. You can pretend you aren't wasting precious time doing meaningless work if the calls come in frequently enough. Unlike everyone else, your cell phone sits boldly faceup on the table beside your work phone. This isn't allowed, but your supervisors have been informed that your mother is dying, so you get to anticipate bad news while you work. It doesn't ring, thankfully, and so you answer phone calls about missing jeans and T-shirts instead.

You have a couple options for obtaining information about your mother from afar. Several of your besties are still in the area. Ellen calls often and knows everything. One week during your sophomore year of college, when your mother was between places, Ellen took her in. Ellen had a husband, a one-year-old son, and a small apartment, so the situation made you sweaty. If your mother overstayed her welcome, it could ruin your friendship with Ellen or impact her marriage. Despite your mother's sweet efforts to keep the house clean and share her food stamps, Ellen said her husband was quick to ask when she planned to leave. Your mother had him on edge, with her loud prayers and her lectures on the dangers of marijuana after she sniffed it on his clothes. You and Ellen both laughed at this. Ellen refused to put her out. You were grateful, embarrassed, relieved. Thankfully, your mother left on her own for a new apartment a few days later.

Last week, you asked Ellen if she could visit your mother in hospice. She said of course, and packed her now five-year-old son and three-year-old daughter into the car for the ride. A text update arrived two hours later. Your heart skipped a beat at the blurry image: your mother on a bed with Ellen's kids in her lap, beaming like nothing was wrong. Their little bodies obscured your view of anything other than your mother's grinning face, maybe a bit less full. You weren't sure what to make of it. Ellen's follow-up text said your mother was in good spirits. You remain unsure.

Shani, your sixth-grade bestie, also still lives in Decatur. You think it's best to keep sending visitors to your mother, to keep getting information. Shani agrees wholeheartedly to go. You sit at work uselessly with your headset on, cell phone faceup. Waiting for a call on either phone. Dreading both.

The customer comes first. With one finger, you type a combination of letters and numbers that she reads to you at a snail's pace. You imagine Shani going through the steps of visitation. Seeing whatever Ellen saw. Maybe she'll send a picture of them smiling too. Instead, your phone vibrates with a text. Even though you're allowed to look, because of the circumstance, it still feels wrong when you open the message.

You should come home.

The sentence fills you with terror. You give your supervisor a look and say you need your fifteen. She gives a sympathetic nod, and you disconnect the customer without a thought. You call Shani back as you walk toward the elevators. Listen in silence while she describes your mother's appearance: "She's very thin. I combed her hair and greased her scalp for her." Your chest swells at this tender act. She reiterates: "You should come home."

Being unable to afford the ticket feels like a shallow excuse. Especially when your other excuse is that you're too busy with work. Both things are true, though not unfixable.

You'll hate yourself if you don't make this happen. But after years of watching your mother call the numbers on her Rolodex for money, you hate asking for help. You freeze in anxiety at the thought of being perceived as needy, incapable. The fear that it's true.

It seems entirely logical to ask your sister, but because you both grew up the same, you hate asking her the most. A couple of your aunts have offered you a ticket via email. You haven't responded. If you wait too much longer, it won't be that you can't but that you didn't.

Mama flat out said it once: *Don't come back here. You focus on your stuff.* It had been a reprieve she probably knew you needed. To understand it was okay to keep running forward as hard as possible. She couldn't deny that; she'd been running her whole life. You came up north to be someone free. Now you feel more chained than ever. Would she blame you if you couldn't make it back?

You should come home.

The sentence replays in the back of your head as you light a second cigarette on this fifteen-minute break. It replays when you stomp out the third one and swipe your key card back into the building. Your brain empties as the elevator carries you up, drops you off on the floor with your cubicle space in it. You take mind-numbing calls. Someone ordered a size 12 and it doesn't fit like their other 12s. A girl's package was delivered to her old address. A mother's baby clothes came stained. You process every problem except your own.

The next day, you have a comatose hang with your friend Elan. He throws a basketball up and down in his living room while some movie he told you was good plays on the television. Last year the two of you binged grainy episodes of *The Larry Sanders Show*, using the show to keep the friendship going after the theater school split you apart. You have a secret handshake together and platonic sleepovers. He's a safe space. When he asks what's the matter you tell him in a rapid but monotone voice, all the words rushing together. The cancer. Your mother is in hospice and you aren't sure when or if you can see her.

Elan makes a generous offer to buy you the plane ticket. He says there's no way he could sit by while you don't get to see your mother; he doesn't say it, but this could be the last chance. Your first instinct is to decline the offer, but your mouth doesn't move. You've trailed behind him at Target while he spent an allowance his parents sent from Pasadena. Placing a new bookshelf, a lamp, snack food, and a pack of white tees into the cart. You marveled at the concept of an *allowance*. The basic comforts you're allowed when you come from a stable home. You felt underprivileged in every way.

He is offering his help, not from pity but from empathy. You are grateful for your friends. After what feels like the length of the movie, you nod okay, quickly wiping tears from your eyes before they fall, and he reaches for his laptop.

South

Hello!
My name is Erika Simpson!
You may know me as family, friend, or
Sallie Simpson's daughter,
but my dream is to be known as a

☆SUPERSTAR!☆

The good news is, I've just been accepted as
one of just 52 selected actors and actresses to
attend DePaul University's theater conserva-
tory in Chicago!!

✈ ✈ ✈

I'm so excited to go off to college and begin my
new journey, but I need your help!
The price for tuition, room & board in the big city,
plus travel, books, and school supplies is adding up!
Could you send any resources to help support
my dream?

This was red-cheeks embarrassing. What no one tells you about
being accepted into a prestigious institution is that you have to

figure out how to get there—and pay for it—yourself. Mama said I was going! No matter what it takes. She made a three-fold pamphlet with one of my hand-on-hip mall pictures on the front flap and filled it up with my story: my various performances at school, the summer theater program at the public library, and my love of being onstage at church. She used lots of exclamation points and decorated with a plane, microphone, and stars from Word's clip art. We mailed it to each of Mama's nine brothers and sisters and every friend in her address book. All that for me. The sentiment of it made me warm, seeing Mama's love for me in action.

Samantha had earned all types of scholarships with her straight As and went to college on a full ride. I felt guilty for being comfortable with Bs and not thinking of the long run. Mama said people needed help to go to school all the time, and that it wasn't too late for me to apply for financial aid. On weekends, she made me sit down at the computer and start typing. Just like her nights searching for grant money online, she made me search for scholarships I could write an essay to win, and encouraged me to share my testimony. "Don't forget your mommy has can-cer," she'd say in a singsong voice, like this wasn't always in the back of my mind. She'd had a month of chemotherapy, and we hoped her latest bout of cancer would be declared remissive soon.

We let the church know I needed God's help via their wallets. Mama showed the pastor's wife my acceptance letter and fund-raising pamphlet, making sure to ask solemnly for her prayers. In return, she sent a collection plate around the congregation after morning announcements.

We got sixty dollars from the church plate and maybe three

hundred dollars from the pamphlet Mama mailed around. I walked the stage and got my high school diploma, and by the end of summer everything came together to get me to college. My essay writing earned me a scholarship that paid out incrementally to the school. For travel funds and school necessities, Mama made me get a ten-thousand-dollar private loan and a credit card the millisecond I turned eighteen. It was enough to cover the first semester, and we agreed to worry about the next one when the time came. We packed the Buick tight with all my books and clothes and headed to Chicago.

The drive was nice at first. We played the same music we listened to on trips taking Samantha to Kenyon. The Temptations' greatest hits filled the car, followed by Smokey Robinson and the Miracles, some Ciara if I waited patiently.

Mama got nervous as the highways got bigger, louder, faster. We started snipping at each other over the paper directions we printed off Yahoo. There were road closures and orange cones, and the overhead sign kept flashing thirty miles to The Circle, twenty miles to The Circle. We grew increasingly anxious, increasingly country, as we wondered what The Circle was, if we were already stuck in it, if another car was gonna hit us. "They could be drunk," Mama half whispered, her reasoning for all roadside chaos, even in the middle of the day.

We made it to campus by four o'clock, aware that the move-in amenities would disappear at 5:00 pm according to the welcome letter that came in my acceptance packet. Mama wanted to find the student center first. She said someone ought to be able to show us around. After deciphering city signs and printed road maps all day, she wanted to feel like someone other than Jesus was taking the wheel. We parked outside a building with a statue of a white man pounding his fist in front of it, which left me feeling uneasy.

The student center blasted air-conditioning throughout its tall interior and boasted large televisions and corkboards with flyers for campus events. The café inside was filled with yoga mat girls and students on laptops visiting invite-only Facebook. After several minutes of us looking confused, a round white security guard offered to be our guide. Finally, a show of friendliness.

Mama and I radiated relief. We were fiending for some southern hospitality to calm our spirits. The man gripped his gunless belt and motioned for us to follow him. He said he'd been working here for over a decade and pointed to the upper levels where I could use my meal plan. Before we could think of a question, he gestured in the direction of student housing, the library, the music school, and the English building. He told us where to get a parking permit and where the freshman orientation would be held. If there was something to know about the university, he knew it.

While we paused in front of the elevators, Mama squeezed my shoulders. "Everything's all right now, baby. We made it. You're exactly where you're supposed to be."

The security guard smiled. "What are you coming to study?"

I puffed my chest proudly. "I'm going to The Theatre School. I want to be an actress."

He shook his head and gave a disbelieving chuckle. "You'd better choose a different career, sweetie. They don't keep black folks around there." The elevator doors opened and he waved for us to board with him, acting as if he had just relayed another boring fact. We rode in silence up to the student affairs office. I pretended my whole world wasn't crashing down inside me. At Towers High School I was a legend, a star, voted Most Likely to Succeed. Here, I was just black.

"Fuck him," Mama whispered to me, holding her chin up even higher, commanding mine to rise with it. I zoned out for the rest of the time Mama got information. My eyes didn't focus until we were safely back in the Buick, circling the campus to find my dorm.

Not one young man held the door open while Mama and I dragged boxes and bags into the dorm. It felt even more embarrassing because we were moving in late, so there wasn't as much of a bustle. Just us, sweating and confused.

Mama spent the night with me, which is more than my sister got when she went to junior college. My roommate didn't show, so Mama camped out on her twin XL, smacking gum and greasing her scalp with Blue Magic while going over how conniving all the people we met were. They were playing games, inviting me to the school but not offering enough money, fake diversity. "Then wanna grin all in your face," she sneered. Her at-home behavior felt jarring in the foreign dorm space, and I was anxious for her to leave so I could start a new identity.

But when she pulled off in the Buick the next morning, I was a wreck. The sight of her waving goodbye, headed back south without me, upturned my whole world. She was going back to the narrative I was familiar with. I was to stay here, furthering the plot inside the story I chose to start.

My alleged ticket to Hollywood, The Theatre School, was a

dingy brick building. There were whispers of remodeling, but I liked the vibration of history in the black rooms with their thick red curtains. Great people had studied in these very spaces. We were the next generation.

The fifty-two of us were divided evenly into four acting sections—a group of people we would take classes with for the rest of the school year. This was a competition, and it was up to us to prove we belonged here for the full four years by the end of the first. I immediately noticed that there was exactly one black girl and one black boy in each of the four sections. This meant that statistically speaking, if half of the candidates were cut, only four of us would remain in the program next year. It didn't make emotional sense for me to cloak up with another black girl, the threat of being split a nightmare. But wouldn't you know it, I became best friends with the other thick black girl, Brittani. There was no way in hell they'd keep both unconventional-bodied girls over two skinny ones. We held tight to each other anyway, spending every second outside of classes together. In a place like this, you had to have someone to confide in.

The main classes were Acting, Voice, and Movement to Music, accompanied by history and art classes in other buildings. In addition, all freshmen in the program had to work as crew members at the theater downtown for the upperclassmen's plays. It was a lot for me to juggle, especially while getting updates on Mama's cancer cells or overdue bills every other morning on the phone.

In my art history class, they said they'd take us to see a play and do other miscellaneous cultural activities, but we each needed to bring a check for $150 by next week. I laughed out loud, a natural *I ain't got it* response, typical for a class in Decatur if the teacher said bring in money. Because why isn't the school funding it and who has $150 sitting around the house to go see a play? But the Lincoln Park classroom remained quiet. A few people looked back at me in confusion. "Sorry," I mumbled. The next week, every student but me handed the teacher a check as they came into class. I had to whisper to her that I couldn't afford it yet. She told me to take my time and I swallowed back the embarrassment.

This was my first time not having money as a singular person instead of the shy little kid holding my mother's hand. Mama told me to open a new account at the TCF Bank in the student center because they were offering students one hundred dollars for new accounts. All we needed was twenty-five dollars to start, and Mama said to do it while I still had the money. The textbooks' prices were crazy too, and you had to move fast if you wanted to catch a library copy. My ten-thousand-dollar personal loan had dried up, lasting only long enough to get us to Chicago after Mama paid two months of back rent with it. I'd have a student refund check soon—a whopping seven thousand dollars if I could hold tight. Mama made sure to keep me in line via snail mail too.

9-11-07 11:30 pm
Hello Erika,
Just thought I would drop you a few lines before going to bed—just finished washing dishes and watching Bones and House to relax me. It's so good to relax and get a little downtime.

I am glad you liked the package I sent. Thought you might like some what-nots—things that are useful +

practical. That can change your attitude when things get a
little tough.

Remember, college is a time of learning more about
patience. You are in a different city—people don't always
get excited about the things we do and you are constantly
surrounded or interacting with adults from different
cultures. Never let people see you sweat—they prey on
that—you become an easy target—even in the bank.
Knowing God is about having faith—confidence that God
is in control, knows what you need and will provide. Right
on time. God is on time. I am sure you know or have found
this out.

So don't, I repeat don't, be anxious for nothing—that
means not waiting around in banks, western unions
for money. Relax. People must not suspect you are
broke—they start labeling you. Let your $75.00 stay in
the bank over 5 days if you can. Don't let people see you
sweat. We don't panic. That's what it means to rest and
trust in God. Don't forget to study and read your Bible
as you do your textbooks. You don't have to let your
friends see you doing it. Just find a good quiet time.
God will direct you. You've begun hearing him instead.
You'll probably refer to such guidance as your conscious
talking :)

Lighten up. Smile more. Relax. I'm here if you need me.
Even though I might not be able to answer as soon as you
call. I do return important messages.

I am forwarding pictures of the kittens. Shirley told me
since I probably will give them away not to name them. I

*think they are precious—as you are again. Especially since
college. Time flies so much.*

*I wish I had been well enough to help Samantha when
she was in college. She had to help me out a lot of times
or she had to turn to others for help. I am glad God put
people, especially grown-ups, to nurture her. I'm sure he'll
do the same for you. Take care of yourself. Alright. Stay
focused on your dreams. Work hard. It will pay off.*

Love, Mom

I avoided sharing things about my home life as much as possible. One detail would lead to another and then I'd be stumbling awkwardly through what my mother did for a living and all the different places we'd stayed. After years of listening to Mama call up friends from her little black book for help, it hadn't occurred to me that I'd join her rotation once I left for school. One of the most pressing bills was the car payment for the Altima she shouldn't have got.

On a night when Mama felt particularly low, she decided to go to the car dealership and purchase a new vehicle. She'd been rolling in her white Buick LeSabre since we'd arrived in Georgia, and she wanted something new, something sleek, something that matched the stature of who she was outside of money. Dreaming of passing my future driver's license test, I told her I had my eye on a black 2007 Nissan Altima with a start/stop button instead of keys. Wouldn't you know it, she asked to see that car when we got to the dealership.

Even listening to the numbers, it didn't feel like the best decision. Three hundred dollars a month plus the insurance when we were barely making rent. Plus the last time I heard about Mama going to a car dealership, she ended up in jail for a year over a bad check. It didn't feel right at all, but Mama needed a win. She signed the papers and we drove the Altima home that night, me trailing illegally behind her in the Buick.

We already had a looming interest rate awaiting us on the ten-thousand-dollar loan once the year's grace period was up. Then there was the credit card in my name that Mama used for her business expenses and grocery emergencies. She'd already run through my sister's credit, which Samantha had personally and meticulously fixed while in grad school, so mine was next. The card was already maxed out. Now Mama was on the phone at 6:00 am, telling me about the Nissan.

"I fell behind on the car payments because I had to catch up on the rent."

"Mm-hm," I replied sleepily, drifting back toward my dorm room pillow.

"They say they'll repossess the car soon, if I don't put something down."

"Mm."

"Did your refund check come yet?" she asked tentatively, casually.

This woke me up. I felt an inner reluctance, but I didn't tell her any lies. "They said within a few days the money should come."

"Well, I sure could use some help down here. Once you get your books and things of course, if you have any extra to help Mommy out."

"Like what?" I knew she loved me. I knew she would call me

at 6:00 am whether she needed money or not, but it was a strange feeling to be a resource.

"They say I need to pay a thousand dollars to keep the car," Mama admitted.

"A thousand dollars!" I sat up in bed. That wasn't even money for food, medicine, clothes, or bills—just a stupid car. That meant she hadn't paid for three months. She knew better than to let anything hit three months.

"Please, baby. I don't wanna lose my car. It's the only nice thing I have."

I was hesitant to say yes. "How would I even get it to you in time?"

"You'd have to overnight it to me."

Picture this like a montage in *Ocean's Eleven*, Mama's plan the voiceover, because even though my sister would've warned me not to send the money, I do exactly as Mama says:

If the refund is a physical check, take it to the TCF to be deposited. Once it clears, withdraw a thousand dollars in cash. I need you to go to CVS, buy a birthday card, it can be a cheap one. Put the cash inside the card. Don't travel around too much with the money. You never know who's watching and waiting. Once you have the money sealed in the card, take that to the post office and tell them you need to overnight ship. That'll cost 17.99. But this way the money arrives to me by plane and sealed, with signature required on delivery.

The plan went off without a hitch. I mailed her the money before noon, and she had it the next day. Safe and sound. No room for anything extra. This mission was about saving the vehicle. Two days later, my phone rang at 7:00 am. It was Mama, hysterical.

"They took it, Jane!" she said. "They took it anyway!"

"Took what?" My brain wasn't there yet. I figured I wouldn't deal with any panicked calls for at least a week after sending off those ten crisp hundred-dollar bills in a $3.99 *Thinking Of You* card.

"They took the Altima. The man just showed up with a tow truck!"

"How?" If it wasn't one thing it was another with Mama. "Did you give them all the money?" I didn't mean to accuse her, but it was madness. The plan went off without a hitch!

"They told me if I put down a thousand dollars they would let me keep it, but now they say that's just back pay and I can only keep it if I pay the *full* amount."

If a thousand dollars was *back pay* I was scared to ask how much she owed in total. "Do you still have the money then?"

"Listen, Jane, that's what I'm trying to tell you! They took the money and the car. *Left me with nothing!*" she wailed into the phone, half crying, half cursing out the dealership, leaving no space for me to react emotionally myself. I remembered the time we visited Mama's mother at Aunt Linda Fae's house. By then Grandma Nora had dementia, and when the three of us walked in she looked Mama dead in the eyes and screamed, "You ain't got nothing! I'll always have a man and money!" It was the sickness talking, but the smallest part of me wondered, *How did she know?*

My refund coins were gone in the blink of an instant, just to pay off someone else's debt. I understood now why my sister didn't respond to phone calls for money. Mama would probably need help with rent in another week. Right when I needed another bump for winter boots or just to eat with my friends at a place off campus.

"Sorry, Mama," I whispered. "At least you still have the Buick." The car was merely a luxury lost, but we had so little that the basics would probably be next.

By November I was homesick for black folks and familiar streets, but going home for the holidays frightened me because Mama and I collectively could only afford a one-way plane ticket to Atlanta. There was no way of knowing how I'd get back. It could be the end of my college journey over two hundred dollars. Mama said God would make a way, which scared me even more because he was barely making one for her. Plus, unlike the way it worked in the wizarding books, the dormitories closed during the holidays, so I couldn't bunker romantically at the school for two months, nibbling cafeteria snacks under a blanket.

We took the gamble, and I came on home. The grass was literally greener in Decatur, Georgia. I took pictures all around the house, and of the flowers in our front yard, and the kittens we had meowing in the garage. A part of me suspected it was all fleeting. My neighborhood friends came over to film corny YouTube videos about double agents, and my high school gang Le Entourage came over for bathroom photo shoots before trips to the movies.

Mama was still plotting next steps for Freedom Peace. She may not have had an office anymore, but she still had her desk set up in the living room. It was nice to be home, if I could also leave again. After a few contract gigs, she was able to get me a bus ticket back to school. Worst ride of my life. Eighteen hours on a Greyhound, the smell of hot-dog water and weed lingering in the aisles, stopping at every single station and evacuating my seat, always just as I was about to fall asleep, and getting colder with every stop farther north. The journey made me feel like the underbelly of America again. One of those who can't afford to reach for the sky, much less travel through it. My seat was a hundred and fifty dollars cheaper than a plane ticket, though. Once I made it off the city train and back to my dorm, my shoulders relaxed. It was good to be home, but it was better being back, moving forward, not hustling within Mama's dream but toward my own.

The path to actually performing was tedious. For starters, freshmen didn't even touch the main stage. We were tasked with learning all the inner fixings of what it meant to put on a successful production. During the day, we took classes. After dark, we headed to the theater in the South Loop to build sets, sew costumes, and hang lights. We'd race all through the theater to do our backstage chores, then watch the actors flub their lines until upwards of 9:00 or 10:00 pm. I felt the furthest thing from famous. Mostly tired. What if this wasn't leading anywhere? Anxiety plagued me every second.

In Movement to Music, the dress code entailed leggings and socks. Leggings as pants—insane to me! The shapes of our asses and our mismatched socks were exposed, the girls standing opposite the boys in their gym shorts on a padded floor. The teacher would lower the lights, hit play on a boombox, then tell us to move uninhibitedly through the space, interacting with each other only if it occurred naturally.

One of my dormmates, Logan, hated Movement to Music because she was small, so all the boys would pick her up and spin her in a circle every time the music swelled. I did not have that problem. Nobody could pick my ass up more than a couple inches. I feared my underwear showing through my leggings, and I wasn't sure how to move to sound in a way that wasn't dancing. I hated feeling the eyes of the teacher on me. Analyzing. Critiquing. In The Theatre School, you had to remember to be *on*, every second, because you were being judged by teachers and peers alike. Cliques were forming, as were favorites.

In Voice class, we played Zip! Zap! Zop! in a circle, shouting make-believe sounds at each other to warm up. Next we'd unlock our inner feelings through a series of *ha ha mmm ahhhs*. We'd squat down spread-eagle to release our dreaded inhibitions through every orifice. I felt dumb as shit doing this white people stuff. I hated making weird sounds and contorting my body with other people watching. I hated wondering what people thought of me, if I belonged here. I hated—

"Erika? Can you be our example? Everyone else sit down. Erika, I want you to make yourself vulnerable. Think of your family, your safe place, and release."

Oh, brother. I hated this instructor and I was sure she hated me. I was as stiff as a grandfather—old and full of secrets—with a gravitas about me that wasn't earned in years of theater training, but from living life. Everyone could sense I had a story. Voice class was apparently about not only projection of sound but also release of self. And if they expected me to do that, then projection was where it stopped.

I stood in front of my whole section, crouching low, then stretching tall, then throwing my head back, making all the random sounds the instructor asked for. And though syllables were coming out of my mouth, I could tell I wasn't giving the intensity she craved.

"Good," she said, her voice sounding displeased, her hands clasped palm to palm in front of her. "Sit down. Let's see. . . . Can you come up, dear?" Her star pupil—the bohemian girl—squatted down real low, like her knees were made of elastic, and she moaned gutturally from deep within herself. The instructor had her stand tall again while releasing sound, and as her head rose to face the class we saw she was sobbing. Releasing animalistic noises louder and louder until she broke into a wail.

"Excellent! There it is. There!" the instructor gushed, handing the girl some tissues and motioning for her to sit. I frowned as our peers rubbed her back.

Bitch wanted me to cry. I just knew it. Class wasn't class; it was the auctioning block. I swear the instructor had wanted to *feel* my grandma being sold off to the highest bidder. I bet she wanted me to wail out some black pain for her to feast upon. Something she could sell to an audience. I wasn't a bad actress and I definitely wasn't stupid. She loved her bohemian, but I had no doubt she'd adore a little black girl to mine, emotionally. It wasn't gonna be me. Maybe I was saving it for the stage.

The classes where we got to perform were the highlight of the day. The stage was all any of us longed for. I liked improv class because I could be savvy and quick instead of vulnerable, as long as I remembered to "yes, and" and not write the entire scene out in my head after speaking one line. The most important class was scripted, though: Acting.

We did mostly AB scenes, where we chose a partner and read from a slip of paper that listed no names, no instructions, no relationships. Only lines of dialogue from speaker A and speaker B.

You were to play with language and your partner to create a moment. Nerve-wracking if you're a suddenly shy black girl from Decatur, standing across from a chiseled white man from California, four years your senior. I had only seen his type of white men on television.

Overall, I felt I was good in acting class. Half the battle was cold reading and quick memorization. Two things that got me through public school with flying colors. We all made mental notes of which classmates we worked the best with, which ones were instant-tear scene stealers, and which gave the same note like a song on repeat. This information would be important at the end of the year, when it came time for each section to do a group performance of a play. But this semester, our final project before winter break was a solo act.

While my non–Theatre School dormmates agonized over chemistry finals and twenty-page papers, our acting assignment was to perform a one-person show. The *autodrama* was to be a ten-minute performance, starring and written by each student, centering a pivotal moment from their life. There were no other instructions beyond that. I feared what my classmates' "pivotal moments" were compared to the things I went through.

The first image that came to mind was Mama getting arrested in 1998, so I went with that. I knew these white folks wanted to hear something black, so I included the tobacco fields and sharecropping from Mama's childhood, a landscape these northerners probably knew nothing about.

The air in The Theatre School buzzed with preperformance excitement on autodrama day. My friend Jeremy, one of the black actors, breezed past everyone, holding four lamps, their cords dragging around his long legs as he rushed to where his class would be performing. I wondered if I should have brought props.

Our section's autodramas began with a brown-haired boy doing a monologue about drinking ten shots too many as a teenager, and his dad having to come get him from jail. I rolled my eyes in the back of the classroom. The monologues varied in topic and weight. Bohemian girl reenacted screaming out her pain on the top of a mountain. Lucky. I screamed into my pillow at night. It was becoming a trauma competition in my head, which I hated, but I was eager to act my ass off and prove I was talented before the semester ended. It was my turn.

Mama had tricks of her trade and I had some for mine. In all situations I like to go last or second to last. The first person sets the tone—usually poorly, because they don't know how the tone could possibly be set and because they're probably a person who likes to "get it over with," which shows through in the performance. If you go at or near the end, you linger in people's minds. You *become* the tone. And everyone else becomes an opening act.

And so I popped my shit. I crouched down low in the corner of the stage area:

"It begins in the tobacco fields of North Carolina."

I sprang up, moving to the rhythm of my words across the whole stage. Telling the story of Mama's childhood, then leading into mine, acting out Mama getting shoved into a police car. I embodied myself at eight years old. I told as much as comfortably vulnerable, before ending my monologue on a positive note about bright futures. My classmates clapped. I couldn't tell the emotion of the clapping, and I don't think they could either. The room fell silent as they waited for the acting professor to tell them their opinion.

She removed her big red glasses and touched a pen to her face. I waited, chest moving up and down like an athlete after the big game. I tried to catch my breath without opening my mouth. She finally spoke: "Have you ever considered writing?"

My mouth did open then. I muttered something that sounded like *No*. It was a lie of course. What with the fan fiction and gangster novels. But that was my sister's thing, writing. It wasn't part of my plan to become a superstar.

"I want to act," I told her, in case this was a trick question and my staying here came down to what I answered when she asked me directly.

"Acting is a cheap trick. Anyone can do it." The vibe in the room changed considerably as frowns rippled through my classmates' faces. "But writing. Some things can't be taught. And you've got it, kid. Have a seat."

There was one more person after me, but I didn't hear a thing. The professor's comments rang through my ears again and again. *Have a seat* gaining more weight with every second that passed.

Winter break was a relief from the literal and figurative stage. Mama was still hustling around town teaching DUI to get caught up on rent and taking her pills to keep the cancer at bay. The next stressor was that we needed a couple thousand dollars for me to enroll in next semester's classes. Mama instructed me to set an alarm for the morning of enrollment, and get into all my classes before the Hold for Non-Payment blocked my computer from registering. Everything worked out, with a few calls to the financial aid office from Mama, and I took the next Greyhound bus back to college.

Despite the endless poverty antics, I made it through another semester of theater school. I did my best not to shrink my personality in the face of new classes and assignments. The final week was like playing fantasy football. Everyone had their list of who they thought would be cut and who would stay. It was a fun way to forget you were also on the chopping block, but I couldn't participate.

There were too many variables. The voice teacher grimaced virtually every time I opened my mouth. The acting teacher called me a writer to my face and in front of the whole class. My body double bestie was a damn good actress with enough presence to play Mama in any play. What were my pros? Truth of the matter was that I was leaving with less confidence than when I arrived. My natural talent seemed to slip away with every fundamental rule we learned from Chekhov or Stanislavski. I was a *charming* person, one of my favorite inheritances from Mama. Yet our storytelling was hard to weaponize against a full institution.

Whenever I entered a discussion about The Cut amongst my classmates, the air would shift, like I'd just let the smoke out of a hotbox. No vibe left in the car, only suspicious eyes. They'd go from confidently throwing out names of who would stay to shrugging their shoulders and shaking their heads. They probably just named each other as the main characters and placed me in the discard pile.

We all hugged goodbye on the last day with uncertainty. There was no telling who would come back and who would be lost to a little town in the Midwest. Mama picked me up from the airport, now leaning on a wooden cane. The sight gutted me. She was aging every second, and all my hard work and nervousness about the future—our future—now relied on a letter arriving by mail in a month.

It wasn't easy to enjoy the summer. How long did it take to critique fifty-two individual actors? I imagined our headshots spread out on a round table in a dim room, our professors staring dark eyed at the choices with cigars and whiskey. How long does it take for a letter from Chicago to arrive in Atlanta? It took the whole year for me to get adjusted, to understand the competitive nature of the environment, to navigate whiteness. Had I stood out amongst the others or just stood still?

The house phone started ringing. It had begun—people were receiving letters. Good friends called personally with the news. Everyone else was hearsay. *So-and-so is out. Such and such is in.* Some cuts made sense. Some keeps were surprising. I wondered if anyone bet money.

D is in. K is in. That was one black boy and one black girl. A handsome and a skinny. Mama told me to trust in the Lord and let his spirit calm me. I nodded but felt nauseous all the while. The phone rang again. *Jeremy was out. Brittani was in.* There was no way they'd take more than two black girls.

During a regular afternoon, while Mama was writing energetically at her desk, I stood to check the mail and there it was: an envelope from the school. During admissions season I learned a big manila envelope meant *Welcome* and a small white envelope meant *No.* I started to disassociate immediately, somehow making it back inside to show Mama.

"You want me to open it?"

"No!" I snapped, but she already had it in hand, peeling the corners of the envelope with a smile on her face.

Students accepted back to The Theatre School got another three years studying acting under trained professionals, leading up to a showcase in Los Angeles their senior year, where they'd perform monologues for Hollywood agents and have access to a celebrity future. These lucky students also walked away with their dignity and self-confidence.

Mama didn't have a nervous bone in her body. I was Tower High School's Most Likely. I was her daughter, a child of God, and there was no way in hell I wouldn't be selected back for another year of acting school. My face went gray while she unfolded the letter. Three-fold like our homemade brochures.

" 'Dear Erika,' " she began to read, but her voice trailed off. Her smile faded with it. "Oh."

"What, Mama?" I was suddenly hysterical, shouting for the information as if she had withheld it herself all summer, hiding the truth like Aunt Mattie in '98.

Mama handed me the letter and sighed, putting her hand on her hip. "You didn't make it." Her voice was flat. I couldn't tell if she was disappointed in me or in general.

I read the words for myself. *After much consideration . . . Taking into account overall performance . . . We have decided not to continue . . .*

That security guard was right. They didn't keep black people up there. Though I had to add an addendum—they'd accepted back three out of four of the black girls. They just didn't keep me.

"We can fight it. There's an appeal process. Did you tell them that you were also dealing with your mother having *cancer* while trying to participate in their little competition?" Mama huffed.

I did try to appeal it. But it didn't matter how long a testimony I wrote about her almost death as a distraction; they had decided to cut me from the program and would not be budging on the decision. Game over.

My first taste of adult-size failure. All I learned from the past year was that there were no guarantees beyond life's vicious ups and downs. I'd ventured off the beaten path and only gotten beaten. Defeated, I asked the question Mama had been asking God for years. *Why me?*

PART TWO

October

You're the last to grab your suitcase from the overhead compartment and exit the plane, the wheels roll bumpily down the jet bridge. Your mouth tastes like morning breath and everything feels disgustingly familiar. The smell of a well-cooked southern biscuit drifts from the Bojangles in the food court. Two old black women are having a friendly conversation outside the bookstore, motioning with their hands every few moments. The people you pass have plump bodies, like yours, and it makes everyone feel like family.

Hartsfield-Jackson Atlanta International Airport is massive. You head toward the airport train and read the signs for baggage claim and car pickup. The train whizzes into place and you stuff yourself inside with suits and carry-ons and teens coming back from whatever retreat. You avoid thinking about how many times your mother has picked you up from this very terminal in the summers. You avoid thinking about the three days she spent sleeping at baggage claim when things got rough. You avoid thinking about her lying on a hospital bed in hospice. Focus instead on the patent leather on a businessman's shoes.

Shani is waiting right outside the airport, her familiar face a relief. She brought her girlfriend, Sarah, who is usually large and talkative but right now stays in the driver's seat of the camel-colored Honda, staring forward. All you can see are the pigtails peeking out from her baseball cap, her hand resting idly on the steering wheel. She seems frozen. You wonder why she won't turn to look at you.

Shani's dimpled cheeks interrupt your thought spiral as she comes in for a hug. It's warm and sincere, a coveted embrace from someone you've known since you were twelve.

"Welcome back." Her tone is caught between excitement and grief. You both know that you wouldn't be here if you weren't visiting your mother. And it isn't exactly a visit. You're coming to see if it's true—if she's almost gone.

Shani takes your bag and puts it in the backseat on the passenger side. You sit behind Sarah, who finally offers a greeting. She makes eye contact in the rearview mirror and you make small talk while Shani buckles her seat belt.

As the car cruises down the highway, your cell phone rings. It's your mother. At times you are so sad for what's coming that you forget she's not dead yet. When you answer, she sounds cheerful, like old times, like good times, and the ache in your belly eases.

"Hey, baby. You landed? You here?"

"I am, Mama; I'm gonna see you in a little bit." Your voice sounds happier than you've felt in a long time. It'll be good to see her. Maybe you've been overreacting. Your mother is resilient. She could beat this thing. Hospice buys time for the money on her disability card to collect. Then she could get a nice apartment.

"I'm excited. I have to warn you, though, I'm a little smaller than I used to be. I don't want you to be shocked when you see me. Mommy's okay."

"Okay."

"Will you pick me up some soap, and some lotion, and some Poise pads before you come? I want my Olay soap. I don't like what they have here." She is using a baby voice on you.

"I can do that, yeah." You've come home to baby your mother. Remind her she is loved.

In the background, a nurse enters her room speaking loudly, and she tells you she'll call back. You ask Sarah to stop by Wal-mart, where you'll spend the last of your money on anything your mother needs.

At the store, you place Olay soap and lotion into a handheld basket. Shani and Sarah trail behind you, flirting and checking their phones. In the next aisle, you grab a twenty-count pack of Poise pads and then reconsider. When will she be able to buy more? Tears well up in the corners of your eyes. She has no family nearby to bring her refills or replacements. There's a fifty-count on the shelf for sixteen dollars. If you get the larger size you'll have to put something back. And you haven't even put Cheetos in the cart yet. She deserved Cheetos. She said the facility only served baked fish or bland chicken with a side of cold rice. You're sup-posed to save the day and can't even afford snacks. A tide of ocean water rises inside your skull, threatening to crash.

No doubt sensing a quiet meltdown and the reason why, Shani speaks up from behind you, "I can get the pads, Shirley." The use of your nickname for each other relaxes your mind. You nod. She reaches over your shoulder and takes them from you with the delicacy of a carton of eggs.

As the three of you head toward the checkout, you see a station of fresh flowers. You have never gotten your mother flowers before. There wasn't really an occasion to do so. Weren't they mostly for Valentine's Day? With a decisive hand you reach for an assortment of yellows, before realizing. Flowers are for gravestones too.

Your stomach feels tight for the entire ride. Sarah fumbles with the GPS on her phone, Shani points at signs, and Sarah recalibrates the directions as you sit in the backseat not saying anything. A part of you hopes they never find the way. You imagine Sarah shrugging it off and Shani shaking her head before they drive you back to the airport.

A breakthrough occurs up front. The car turns down a road that looks newly paved, surrounded by willowy trees. You don't know what area you're in, but it feels like you're spiraling toward a hidden place. For a split second you wish you'd taken a cab from the airport instead. Why did you come with company? Should this have been a quiet moment alone with your mother?

Truthfully, you don't have enough money for a cab from the airport. You imagine yourself climbing into a taxi with a sullen look on your face. The driver places your suitcase into the trunk, and you tell him the address, then sit in a pregnant silence until you arrive. You could have stolen the ride. Waited until he pulled up to the hospice and then burst into tears.

You could have told him that your mother, the woman who gave birth to you, is inside all alone. That you had no other way of getting here. Through tears, you could have asked if he'd forgive the fifty-dollar ride for a devastated stranger. He would have understood. He would have told you that his family is back home in another country and that when his mother died two years ago he wasn't able to be there. He would nod in approval and add something cheesy like, *Go be with your mother.* And you'd be able to leave without paying. Maybe you'd have forgotten your suitcase in the hurry to get out of the car.

Your mother would love this show of determination and valor. She'd have retold the story of when she did the same after dropping your sister off at college. You would have listened, grinning and laughing the whole time, as if you weren't there when it happened. You could have done the same thing to get here. But you didn't. And in all honesty, you could not have come alone.

Shani points to a hanging bracket sign that says *Halcyon Hospice* in big cursive letters. You've arrived. It looks like a cottage. The grass is fresh cut and tall plants grow around the yard and by the windows. You remember your mother is inside, and your stomach churns like you're going to vomit up everything you've eaten in the past week. The GPS reiterates that you've reached your destination, and Sarah pulls into a space near the front.

She cuts the power to the engine and removes the key from the ignition.

Shani turns in the passenger seat to look at you, offering a tight-lipped smile. "Ready?"

You are not.

CC: Closed captioning provided by FOX network, 1997
[eerie music plays]

Medieval chandeliers lined with flickering candles hang over a mysterious parlor, illuminating an open-faced tomb against the wall with an ancient mummy inside. A man in a suit enters, bathed in darkness as he comes to stand beside a lamplit desk and a glowing world globe. With a casual hand in his pocket and a quiet knowing, he smiles. "It's time once again to cross over the boundary and beyond belief."

Announcer:

B e y o n d   B e l i e f : Fact or Fiction.
Hosted by Jonathan Frakes.

"We live in a world where the real and the unreal live side by side. Where substance is disguised as illusion. And the only explanations are unexplainable. Can you separate truth from fantasy? To do so you must break through the web of your experience, and open your mind to things . . . Beyond Belief.*"*

Jonathan Frakes:

Faith. A driving force for human beings in the game of survival. A belief in something outside of yourself. Something unseen and unknown. Consider the Bible. The stories contained within its pages are fantastical. Talking snakes, men turned to stone, floods and famine. At the center of it all a benevolent or vengeful God. Just out of sight.

Enter the story of Job. One of God's most faithful servants. A man with a good life and a better family, loyal to the Lord in every way. As it goes, the devil challenges God to a bet that Job will abandon his faith if he suffers. God lets the devil do his worst. He destroys Job's crops, plagues his body with sickness, and kills his children in a fire. Through all this devastation, Job's faith never yields, and in turn, God rewards him with restored health, new land, and even a replacement family.

How do we take this tale? Are our pains a test from God or a trick of the devil? Sallie Carol Simpson is what we'd call one of God's strongest soldiers, suffering from recurring cancer, financial instability, and frequent loss. In this episode, we examine Sallie's life and ask a weighted question. Should she expect a miracle in the nick of time or is the Bible full of fantasy fables?

Tonight you will see stories that walk the border between fact and fiction. At one point they may seem true to you; at the next moment, false. We'll tell you which is which at the end of our show. Of course, there's one thing they'll all have in common: a miracle.

The Power of Love

Charlotte, North Carolina, 1980. Sallie Carol was a bright and proud new teacher at the public high school, just twenty-four years old. She'd loved education for as long as she could remember, first teaching her siblings how to read and write when she was a kid, and now teaching science to ninth and tenth graders. The students loved her. She drew them in with her animated speech and patient understanding.

Dylan, a sophomore, only paid attention for the hour he spent in her class. He eagerly volunteered to draw molecules on the board and test bacteria, and even stayed after the bell to clean. Dylan saw Ms. Simpson as the only light in his dark high school experience. Sallie was glad to help. She believed every student possessed endless potential and loved to watch their minds and smiles expand.

Work was often easier than her personal affairs, something she could quantify and conquer. Back home she couldn't control anything. She'd gotten married quickly to her sweetheart, Steven. Her family hated him, and his family hated her. Somehow that made them more madly in love. But within a few years, he proved to be less than a Romeo when she caught him cheating with a

Juliet from his office. They'd been eating dinner in silence for two days now, and she wasn't sure what to do.

Dylan asked her for help studying after school on Monday, but she told him she had to get home to her husband. Dylan asked again on Tuesday, but she had been too emotionally distraught about the cheating and, without giving any reasons, asked for a rain check. On Wednesday, Dylan didn't bother asking, which relieved Sallie. She could use the time after school to grade a stack of tests. Just as she reached into a file cabinet, she heard someone breathing heavily behind her.

"You should be with me, Ms. Simpson."

"What?" She turned around to see Dylan with his hoodie up, and his hands buried in his pockets, looking sweaty and ill.

"We make each other happy. I want you to be with me."

Understanding hit Sallie slowly, and she shook her head with a shy smile. "I'm your teacher. And I'm married."

Dylan pulled a gun from his pocket and pointed it directly at her. "He doesn't deserve you! I do! I love you! You have to be with me!"

"Dylan . . ." Sallie put her hands up cautiously. "I love teaching you, but I can't—"

"You *can*!" he huffed, pointing the gun harder. "Isn't that what you teach? We can do *anything* we put our minds to, right?" He tapped the gun to his temple. "We leave together or not at all."

"Dylan."

He pointed the gun at Sallie's head, tears in his eyes, and as he went to pull the trigger, the door flew open.

"Sallie?" Her husband, Steven, entered the classroom with a bouquet of flowers.

The gun went off.

The sound echoed through the entire room. When it finally stopped, Sallie opened her eyes, waiting to feel the pain. But the bullet had connected with the file cabinet beside her. Steven's entrance shocked Dylan so much it made his arm waver. When he realized he missed, he dropped the gun and ran from the room, leaving Sallie and Steven staring at each other in disbelief.

*   *   *

Jonathan Frakes:

Did this near-fatal incident really happen? Did an all-seeing God orchestrate for a husband's poor behavior to lead to a perfectly timed entrance—or was it a coincidence? Is Sallie alive today because she's supposed to be or is this whole story too much of a long shot? We'll find out soon.

You enter a housing facility that's nicer than any place you've ever lived, holding flowers in front of your face like you're headed to a blind date. Your friends trail behind like solemn wingmen. The white lady sitting at the front desk asks who you're here to see. You give her your mother's name. Without taking a moment to think she says, "Room three-twelve," and points a fingernail toward the sign-in sheet, which is nestled beside flowers much nicer than your Walmart bouquet. It's strange, checking in to see your mother. Shani signs for herself and Sarah on the lines beneath your name.

Gray-haired people sit on a plush sofa in a living room area to the left. They stare blankly at a television playing *Rush Hour* while a popcorn machine churns out a fresh batch. You find it odd that the smell of the kernels doesn't fill the room. Only sterile scented air freshener. It's too sunny here. Brightness plastered over inevitable darkness.

Shani and Sarah are waiting. You put on a face of false bravado and walk down the hallway toward room 312. A couple nurse ladies amble in and out of rooms carrying toiletries. Every doorway you pass shows the end of a different life. An old woman with big loose curls sits in a wheelchair beside her bed. In a dark room, a shriveled man lies on an elevated bed with tubes and oxygen tanks all around his body. The image makes you anxious enough for the flower petals to tremble in your hands. Room 310 is empty of residents, just two women inside changing the sheets and wiping down surfaces. Someone must have died. You avert your eyes.

Room 312. You take one last ignorant breath before you enter. One final moment as a person with blind hope who can stay in Chicago guilt-free and ignore your mother's calls because more will come.

"Is my mama in here?" You walk into the room with gusto and a voice so jolly it burns your ears. There she is.

"Hey, baby!" She is sitting on a hospital bed in the middle of a room not too different from the hotels you've lived in, beautiful and hollow in a black sweat shirt with her usual bright smile and vibrant energy. Her skin is impeccable. Black has never once cracked. But her cheeks are sunken and her Afro is unkempt, her body thinner than in the pictures that you've seen of her from high school. Your heart slams up against your chest. You want to cry, but instead you hold out flowers.

"Oh, Mama."

She sees right away that you are hurting and reaches for you. "Don't cry, baby; Mama is okay. I told you I got a little thin, didn't I? You didn't believe me. But I'm okay."

You sink down beside her on the bed and into her embrace. There's less of her to hold on to, but it's comforting still.

"Hey, Shani! And Miss Sa-rah!" Your mother releases you, leaning to the left to get a hug from your friends. You busy yourself trying to find something vaselike while they chat. Flowers were a bad idea. They'll wilt fast, an unintentional metaphor for her life. You put the stems in a mug that still has water inside. Beside it is a small balloon on a stick that says: *Feel Better Soon.* Aunt Mattie came a couple weeks ago. Everything else on the table is beige. The cups, the pitcher, the plate. The color of drained life.

"Mama you didn't finish your food." You point to the cold rice and baked fish on an abandoned meal tray.

She makes her classic goofy-faced pouty mouth, and furrows her brow. "That nasty mess. I want a sausage, egg, and cheese biscuit."

Sarah chimes in, "I know that's right, Ms. Simpson. You want them to bring you some real food." Shani and Sarah are seated in the room's two armchairs.

You remain standing. Your mother continues, her signature stream of words another comfort. "They treat me like a child in here. Every time I do anything they want me to *ring the bell.* I'm an independent woman. I've been wiping my own ass for fifty years. I don't need no help now."

"I know that's right, Ms. Simpson." Sarah sounds like a non-playable character in a video game right now.

Shani, the one who's known your mother longer, gently offers encouragement. "They just want to help, that's all. They don't want you to hurt yourself."

"Oh, child, please. They working for that check. I know they getting paid for every week they can keep me in this room."

You can't stop watching her face. It doesn't look all the way like hers. She resembles her father, who was very tall and very thin.

"And they keep it so cold in here. I'm shivering and they bring these thin-ass blankets." She kicks her feet beneath the covers to demonstrate how thin the pink bedspread is. You register that it is not cold in the room, but the thought is replaced with relief that she can still move her legs. The doctors said a long time ago that she would someday be paralyzed, and cancer in the spine does not promise much.

"Be grateful, Mama."

"I am grateful; I just want to get back to work. It's been nice getting some rest and getting off my feet but I have things to do. I want to finish my ministry."

You register something again. A sense that the things she's saying don't make sense.

"I have to use the restroom." Your mother says this in a hurry, as if she hasn't much time. She uses the bed rail to pull herself up. As her feet touch the floor, you notice her gray sweat pants look a size too big. She struggles to stand, and you walk over to help her.

"No, I got it. They want me to push the button for help, but I can get myself to the bathroom." She walks in that rigid, cautious way that babies walk when they're trying to make their legs go. As she inches toward the bathroom, you create a protective halo with your arms around her body. Just in case. She makes it to an elevated toilet, barely gets her sweats and underwear down before you hear the sounds of release and she gives an excited grin. "I made it!"

You close the door behind her and try to gulp down the sinking feeling in your chest that she did not seem embarrassed. Strangers in this hospice have been helping her to the restroom all this time. She is infantile.

You can't bear to catch Shani's eye, or that of Sarah, who is giggling casually. Maybe you should be alone with your mother now. She hobbles out of the bathroom, making noises of pain and muttering quietly. You help her back onto the bed and she doesn't resist. She asks you to adjust her pillows against her back, and to raise the bed up a little higher with the remote control. You can't imagine that just two months ago she was hustling to catch a bus with two suitcases in tow and not a place on earth to go. You are nervous as hell.

"Mama, I'm going to walk Shani and Sarah to the car and then come back so we can hang out by ourselves a little bit, okay?" Your friends stand immediately, as if this was all planned. Shani gives your mama a tight hug and says that she will see her tomorrow. Sarah follows suit. You are about to walk them out when your mother calls you back.

"Hand me my purse before you go, baby. I need to get my medicine out." She gestures at the top of the highest shelf in the room. It's built-in storage between the bed and the bathroom.

"How did you get your purse so high?"

"I'm not risking nobody stealing my purse. These nurses come all in the room at night when you're asleep and try to go through your stuff looking for money. I ain't dead yet. And I ain't stupid."

Your mother has always been distrustful of others, so her words are no surprise. Her purse is ridiculously heavy and worn and black, and you place it on the side of her bed.

"I'll be right back, Mama."

You aren't really walking your friends out. They're already seated in the car, texting and smiling to each other in polite conversation. This is not happening to them. Not yet. You lean against the car's back bumper, pull a pack of Marlboro Reds from your jacket pocket, and light one slowly. The first drag feels like it is saving your life, but then it's not. The smoke acts as a physical representative for the thoughts that have been spinning inside your brain. You're so drained already.

The plane ticket you got is for two days. You have a little more time today, and time tomorrow, and then you will be back in Chicago where nothing will feel as real as it does here. You try to blow the cigarette smoke up and outward so that the smell doesn't cling to your clothes with the sadness. You don't want to upset your mother, and you don't want her to know that she's upsetting you.

Trial and Execution

Atlanta, Georgia, 2005. Sallie's eighth-grade students looked at bacteria under microscopes and completed their worksheets while she walked around observing. After more than twenty years of teaching science, she was an old pro.

As class time dwindled down, Sallie stood behind the lab demonstration table to collect assignments. Students ambled up one by one to hand in their papers, but a boy named Marcus hovered near her shoulder. "Your Afro looks lopsided, Ms. Simpson."

She ignored him, instead reminding the class about next week's assignment. The boy remained beside her, smirking in her direction.

"Let me fix it." He reached in his back pocket, eyes trained on his teacher.

Sallie tensed, her mind transporting back to her classroom in North Carolina, when a young boy looked at her just as strongly before pulling a weapon. She shook the memory away. "Go back to your seat, Marcus!"

His eyebrows furrowed and he smacked his teeth. "Let me fix it!" He took a step closer to Sallie, and before she could respond, yanked his hand from his jeans, revealing a black pocketknife, speeding toward her.

Yelping loudly, she flinched away and threw a hand up to protect herself, connecting with something solid. The object he was holding fell to the floor.

Marcus clutched the side of his face. "No, you didn't just hit me! She slapped me, y'all! Ms. Simpson just hit me!"

Sallie shook her head. "He had a—!" But when she looked to the floor, the sight made her mouth fall open. What she thought was a knife was merely a plastic hair pick, the black power fist that formed the handle looking up at her.

The students around them started *ooohing* like she was in trouble, and she put both hands in the air, waving for silence. "My mistake. Calm down, everybody." The bell rang before she could finish. Her eighth graders filed out with wide eyes, looking back and forth between her and Marcus. He stood frozen, eyes locked on her, hand still clutching his cheek like he was protecting evidence.

The consequences came quickly. A council was formed and a trial was held by the next week. With Sallie's career on the line, it was her word against her student's. He claimed that he politely offered her a hair pick and she slapped him across the face. While this wasn't true, Sallie didn't want to sound crazy, so she omitted from her testimony that she thought he had a knife. She restated that he was heckling her about her hair, then entered her personal space, which shocked her, and she absentmindedly swung her hand backward.

The council, more concerned that the boy's parents might threaten to sue, fired Sallie. She had to clean up her desk and turn in her badge, this moment now staining the rest of her career. She would have trouble finding another teaching job after this, and she and her girls would begin to struggle again.

Two weeks after the trial, on a Saturday, while Sallie flipped through the newspaper in search of work, her old middle school appeared on the television in front of her. To Sallie's surprise, a mug shot of her former student Marcus popped up. The anchorwoman said that there was a brutal attack. The young man pulled a knife on one of his teachers after she handed him back a test with a failing grade. The teacher was rushed to urgent care but unfortunately did not survive. The newspaper fell from Sallie's hands.

* * *

Jonathan Frakes:
What really happened in that classroom? Did PTSD from the past just happen to protect her future, or did God give Sallie a premonition that would keep her safe? Was unjustly losing her job part of a larger blessing, or are we stabbing in the dark?

You head back inside and hear a commotion coming from down the hall. A nurse is trying but failing to make her raised voice sound calm. You start speed walking once you remember room 310 is empty, so the only commotion from that area would be from your mother.

"Are you the daughter?" The nurse is a thick older black woman with short brown hair and glasses. She looks stern and impatient. "Are you the youngest one or the oldest one?"

"That's the baby!" your mother shouts, sitting on the bed looking mad as hell and more frazzled than ever.

"Can you please tell your mother to hand over any and all medications that she is self-prescribing?"

"That's my baby daughter. She doesn't know anything," your mother replies, not once breaking eye contact with the nurse. Wide-eyed and frightened, you can't bring yourself to speak. A twenty-four-year-old baby indeed.

"Ma'am, you cannot take medication that we don't know about. We must be aware of all medications."

"*Y'all are trying to kill me!* I need that medication! My doctor gave me that medication and told me to take one dose every two days!"

"Ma'am." The nurse is talking to you now, holding out a needle and syringe. "When I walked in, your mother was giving herself a shot of this in the belly." She calls it by its intricate medical name before continuing, "Now it's *fine* if she would like to continue a treatment, but we must know about it so we can administer the correct doses."

Your mother is furious and has somehow risen from the bed. "I have a tumor in my stomach!" She lifts her shirt up to reveal a lump with blackened skin above her belly button. A similar lump forms in the center of your throat and she continues, "My doctor gave me those syringes to help reduce the swelling and it is the *only* thing that has helped! You people are not gonna come in between me and my healing. I am not some drug addict shooting up. I taught alcohol and drug abuse for *twenty-six years*!" She emphasizes every single syllable so that you see her teeth when she says the word "six." "I will not be treated like I'm uneducated."

The nurse looks at you and then back at your mother.

You manage to speak: "I can't tell her to do anything." At this, your mother makes a triumphant face.

"You told me you weren't going to act up today, Ms. Simpson." The nurse looks over the rim of her glasses with a hand on her hip. "You told me you'd be good because your daughter was coming." She walks toward the door and takes the syringe with her. "I'm going to trust you don't have any more of these in your purse. The next time you need one, we will administer it. No one is trying to stop you from being comfortable. You just need to let us know." She exits.

You notice her use of the word "comfortable," rather than "healed." Your mother slowly descends back onto her bed, as if she has used the last of her energy to abolish the nurse.

"They got me trapped here," she says.

You help lift her legs back onto the mattress and take a seat in one of the armchairs. Your mother continues, staring straight ahead, "They want me to die in this room. But no. I have a doctor's appointment on Monday and I am walking straight down to the bus stop and taking myself to Grady Hospital. I'm gonna tell my doctors I want to continue treatment. I will live. I'm not giving up. God says I have work to do. I'm not spending another month on this bed."

You are sadder than you have ever been in your life. Your mother's spirit is more resilient than her body. You don't know how to respond.

"Can you go tell them to bring me some more water? I need to take my vitamins so I can stay strong. And tell them to turn the heat up in this cold-ass room." She's staring at you now. "Can you get me some more water, baby?" You see the outlet she's offering and you take it, nodding as you stand.

You grab the beige water pitcher and head to the front desk where three women greet you: the nurse who just left and two white women with clipboards and social worker smiles.

"You're Ms. Simpson's daughter, yes?" the redheaded woman asks. You nod. She and the blonde one nod at each other and smile and check things off on their clipboards. The redhead continues, "We want to ask you a couple of questions."

"Is there water up here? My mom said she wanted more water. And that her room is cold." You talk to all three of them so that they will not talk to you individually.

"I'll get your mama some water." The black nurse reaches for the water pitcher and excuses herself down the hall.

"We have a *Vernell Bellamy* on file for first contact, is that right?" The blonde is smiling at you again.

"Um, yes. I guess. That's her sister. Her older sister. My aunt Vernell." These things are obvious, but you say them anyway. "Maybe call Aunt Mattie first. That's her younger sister. But she's the best for handling situations." You realize that you're talking about people in their fifties and sixties, and that it doesn't matter anymore who's the youngest or oldest.

The blonde hands you a slip of paper. "Would you mind writing her number down? Or anyone else that we can contact?"

You awkwardly fish for your cell phone in your jacket pockets while they watch. The redhead clears her throat. "Also . . ." She pauses before continuing in a tender tone, "Your mother seems unhappy here? I know she tends to get upset with the nurses when they try to help her out."

"My mother is very independent." Why has your voice gotten so loud? Why are you so defensive?

"And we definitely understand that," the blonde says. "Does she suffer from any mental issues? I see here she's bipolar, but it feels a bit worse than that." She taps her pen against the surface of her clipboard while she speaks. You decide she's ugly.

"She . . ." Your mind screams for you to say nothing. Mama raised you to trust no one like on *The X-Files*. Yet your mouth keeps talking. "She may be borderline schizophrenic as well. She showed the signs. Of that." You feel disgusting, like you should not be saying these things to anyone but your sister via telephone. This is a betrayal of your mother, who's only a few feet away in a hospice bed.

Red's brow furrows and she takes notes, still nodding and half smiling. "Yeah"—a soft coo—"I know whenever we visit she talks about going back to work? She says she wants to get back into the community?"

"Yeah." You whisper coo right back, unsure how you feel about this or what to think of these women and what they're implying.

"I'm just worried that she doesn't have a good grasp of what's going on. She doesn't seem to be comprehending," Blonde says.

"Well"—you are absolutely defensive now—"she's dedicated to her work. It's what drives her. So, yeah. She's feeling trapped here." This is a jab at the hospice, at these two women who keep nodding and smiling when all you wanted was for someone to get your mother some goddamn water. "She says she wants to go to her doctor's appointment, but everyone keeps telling her to lay down."

Blonde is at full attention now and the smile is fading. "The doctor's appointment on Monday?"

You nod.

Blonde nods back. "We aren't keeping anyone from leaving. We are more than happy to drive our patients to the doctor, but there has to be an actual appointment."

A jab. "What do you mean?"

"We've called her doctor and he's confirmed that there is no appointment on Monday. Or ever. He's told your mother that there is nothing left to do. The cancer's spread throughout her blood and into her spine. And now that it's gotten to her brain, we think that she's getting confused."

You are struck. Blonde has revealed something that you did not know. *The cancer has spread to her brain.* You suppress any outward show of emotion, but on the inside your heart's shredding into pieces and drifting down through your insides.

She's been getting confused. There is no doctor's appointment. You don't know how to respond. You picture tiny maggots chewing at the parts of her brain that she is the proudest of. Eating at her education, her memories. Telling her things that aren't true. Red speaks up.

"Your mother is welcome to stay. But we're thinking she may be a better fit at the Catholic hospice in Atlanta. It's closer to the Braves stadium and they take their patients to games every week, so she doesn't have to feel *trapped*. And the nuns can pray with her." She pauses. "Do you want to schedule for her to be moved there next week?"

"What?" You feel like an infant, barely able to understand.

"We can arrange for her to be picked up. Or do you think she'll want to go stay with your aunt Vernell or your aunt Mattie?"

Red is waiting for an answer, but you're too little to make decisions like this. *The cancer has spread to her brain. She's getting confused. There is no doctor's appointment. The doctor told her there was nothing else they could do.* The information is consuming you.

"I . . . I don't know. She doesn't want to go to North Carolina. She likes it here."

Blonde hugs her clipboard close to her chest. "Okay. Well, she doesn't have family here, right? You stay in Boston?"

"No. That's my sister. I live in Chicago."

"Right, okay. We thought you were the oldest one. So would you suggest moving her to the other hospice? Say, on Monday?"

"I can't. My sister will be here next week. We couldn't come at the same time. I'm too young to . . ." You are starting to freak out, and it's showing. Why didn't they just call Aunt Vernell if they had her phone number? What else is your mother getting confused about? If they said she could stay, then why were they so persistent about the other hospice? And where did the black nurse go?

Red places her hand on your shoulder in a practiced gesture of comfort. "We don't mean to overwhelm you. We're just trying to get as much information as possible while someone from her immediate family is here. We can definitely speak with someone else from the list. Enjoy your visit." Just like that, they retreat, leaving you with everything that they have told you.

When you enter your mother's room again, she's flicking through the channels on the television across from her bed. "Did they bring you water?"

"Yeah, they brought it. The nurse playing nice now. She came in here fluffing my pillows and asking if I was warm enough. She knows she was wrong for taking my medicine."

"Yeah." You say it in the same cooing voice that the women used on you, but it is the only tone that you can think to speak in. "Hey. Do you want to see some pictures on my phone?"

"Sure, baby. Show me your pictures."

You wrestle the bag of Cheetos from the Walmart bag and she delights, both of you choosing to move past the last hour and enjoy the next.

Breathing Room

Goldsboro, North Carolina, 1988. Sallie was scared, she must admit. Despite her brain's effortless gathering and passing on of knowledge, she'd been having frequent headaches and her vision grew dimmer every day. That's when the doctor delivered the horrifying news. She had a brain tumor. Not only that, its location between her eyes and near the nasal passage made surgery extremely difficult, if not impossible. She decided to attempt the procedure anyway, praying that God would keep her vitals strong throughout the ordeal.

As she lay on an operating table, waiting to be wheeled into surgery, she continued praying quietly for herself, for her young daughter, Samantha, and for the survival of her marriage through sickness and health. A female nurse came in right after Sallie said, "Amen," and gave her a formal nod before wheeling the table into surgery. The woman told her to count backward from ten. "Jesus, Jesus, Jesus," Sallie whispered instead, slipping into blackness as the anesthesia took her under.

Several hours later, she came to in a dimly lit hospital room. Her breathing felt labored and her skull ached. It was hard to keep her eyes open. She wanted to drift back to sleep so the pain would stop.

Suddenly a bright light shone into her eyes. She fluttered her eyelids open and closed against the glare until a friendly face appeared. A black male nurse looked down at her, smiling as bright as the light that seemed to illuminate him from behind. With a click of his thumb, she realized there was actually a small flasher in his hand.

"Wakey, wakey, Ms. Simpson. How do you feel?"

She could barely open her mouth. "Head hurting."

The kind-faced man nodded. "Can you stay strong for me, Ms. Simpson? You gotta hold on a little longer."

Sallie struggled to respond, each breath more difficult than the last, so she nodded. The man looked so familiar. His eyes and mustache. Like family.

"It's not time to go to sleep yet, Sallie. You got more teaching to do. And way more learning." He winked at her before pressing a button on her bedside.

She let her eyes drift closed. They were so heavy. The man told her to be strong, but the pull of sleep called to her like a siren.

"Oh, Ms. Simpson!" Her lady nurse from earlier rushed into the room, eyes wide at whatever stats were showing on the medical machines. "I'm not sure how your oxygen levels got so low." She hurriedly adjusted the settings and straightened the cords attached to Sallie's arms.

After a few seconds, Sallie's lungs filled with oxygen and she took hungry drinks of air.

The nurse let out a relieved breath and patted Sallie's hand. "Thank God you were able to reach the help button in time."

Still gathering air and her thoughts, Sallie shook her head. "No. The male nurse helped me." She had to tell him thank you. She could have died right in this room.

"What male nurse? It's just me and Ms. Gina tonight, darling. But don't worry. We'll keep an eye on you." The nurse gave her a reassuring smile before turning the lights out and leaving.

Sallie could only blink at the ceiling. No male nurses? Then who had just saved her life?

* * *

Jonathan Frakes:
Was Sallie once again spared by a higher power? Or was the tumor in her brain playing tricks on her psyche? If so, how do we explain the help button being pressed? Was there an angel in the outpatient room or are we telling a devilish lie?

Announcer:
We'll find out which of our stories tonight were fact and which were fiction when Beyond Belief *returns. . . .*

Before you left the hospice last night, your mother gave you a list of errands. You must pick her medicine up from a CVS in Atlanta. It has to be a specific one or else they won't give you the Flonase that she needs to keep her nostrils clear for breathing. Then go to the post office and get her mail. She's expecting a letter from Aunt Vernell and a notice from her lawyers about a new settlement she is filing against the hospital. And lastly, go to her storage unit at the U-Haul off Memorial Drive. She needs fresh clothes to wear, because she isn't sure about the laundry at the hospice, and she wants her big Bible, full of her handwritten notes. You told her you'd make it happen.

Shani waits in the car while you run into CVS. Your voice comes out mouse quiet to the man at the pharmacy counter: "I'm picking up for Sallie Simpson. She's not able to pick up." He doesn't investigate the statement, just hands you the prescription. You sign on an electric line and head back to the car. Easy.

The post office is seven minutes down the street by car. Your mother would have to catch two separate MARTA buses to make it there from the CVS. Which she did, probably every other day, on swollen feet. Shani leaves the car running while you go inside for your mother's mail.

You and Mama came to this plaza every weekend when you

were in high school. First the post office and then to T.J. Maxx to catch the deals. The cashiers would greet her when she came in, "Hey, Ms. Simpson!," and she would wave back saying, "Those my girls!" She knew everybody's backstory. Patricia, who left her boyfriend of nine years after three kids and twelve beatings. Ms. Jocelyn, who went to school at night after her shifts to get her nursing degree. Teisha, who was a former student of hers from Brown Middle School. When they found the time to get this deep over a checkout counter you had no idea, but they knew all about her too. While she paid for the day's findings, whoever was working the register would gush, "You must be her baby girl."

You stand in front of a row of familiar mailboxes, fingering the numbers on each, trying to remember which one is your mother's. 1886? 1868? The key won't open the ones you try. You resign yourself to standing in line, nervous they won't give you her mail without an ID. A black lady postal worker waves you forward.

"Hello. I need to pick up the mail for my mother." The woman frowns and your hands shake. "She can't come. She's in hospice."

"Oh dear." The woman sounds much nicer than you imagined. "What's her name, sweetie?"

"Sallie Simpson."

The woman's eyes widen and she takes a step back. "No. You not talking about Ms. Simpson? Is she okay? You must be her baby girl."

It feels like someone has punched you in the gut, and it's taking everything not to sink down to the floor. Of course she knows your mother and of course she knows you. "Yes."

"Oh no. I was wondering where she had been. Your mama usually comes in here smiling and waving her wooden cane and we get to talking about everything." She pauses again. "I hate to hear she's in hospice. Cheryl! This is Ms. Simpson's daughter. She says Sallie is in hospice." The woman standing at the counter space nearest to her makes a worried expression.

"Hold on, baby, let me get her mail. It's box eighteen-seventy-eight." She scuffles off, leaving you to sit with the quiet appreciation of your mother's little life, then the grief that she's not currently living it.

The postal worker returns with seven envelopes and then grabs at your wrist. "Please will you tell her to call me? My name is Evelyn." She scribbles her name and number down onto a scrap of torn envelope from behind the counter and hands it to you. "Please tell her to call me, okay?"

The last errand is the U-Haul facility. Shani stops the car in front of the leasing office so you can get pointed toward the right row of storage units. Your mother said a woman named Francine who worked here was a proper *witch*. She said the woman never let it slide when she needed to pay late and was probably going through her things after-hours. You walk into the cramped office to a gray-haired black woman at the desk. A table fan is pointed directly at her face. Her eyes are trained on a television in the corner playing an episode of *Maury*.

"Welcome to U-Haul." Her eyes only sort of pull away from the TV screen.

"Hi. I was trying to find my mother's storage unit? Thirteen-fifty?"

She stares at you full on now with a bemused grin. "Don't tell me you Sallie Simpson's daughter?"

There's that punch in the gut again. "Yes."

The woman crosses her arms now. "So you the baby girl, huh? I was wondering where your mama was at. I ain't seen her shuffling around. She usually come over the hill with her suitcase and her cane looking mad as hell."

You can't help but laugh, because it sounds true. "That's her."

"Your mama got two moods: she either mad as hell or she your best friend." You both laugh now. This must be Ms. Francine.

"That sounds right. She told me you were a witch." You say it just to see how she'll react.

"Mhm. Yeah, she also say I been stealing her stuff. I tell her, 'Ms. Simpson, what in the *world* would I need with whatever you keeping up in that storage unit?' And she get real mad then." Ms. Francine shakes her head. "She something else. But she talk about her smart girls all the time. Where she been anyway?"

This is the part you have been dreading. "She's not feeling well. She's in hospice right now."

"Oh no. Well, I really hope she gets better, okay?" She gives you a tight smile, and the joy you felt from the conversation dulls. "Anyway, her storage unit is across the street."

Unit located, you slip the key into the tiny padlock at the bottom of the orange door. It doesn't seem like much protection for people's valuables. But it may not be very valuable if it's in a storage unit. With a good tug, the door springs upward. In your mind there'd be neat rows of labeled boxes, maybe a lamp leaning casually against a TV set, and an open shoebox housing family photos. Not quite.

The desk that your mother kept in the living room sits against the back wall, buried beneath trash bags filled with clothes and stacks of boxes that have been packed and repacked with different-colored tape. The boxes pile all the way to the ceiling. Old suitcases lean against the side wall and grocery bags of underwear rest atop those. It all looks like junk.

You dig around in a pink backpack, fighting tears while you grab her Bible and a few shirts that look clean enough to wear. Your eyes scan over a grocery bag that looks like a survival kit, with a travel-size toothpaste and deodorant, a bar of hotel soap, and a packet of ramen. You take a deep breath and wipe your face before returning the bag to its resting place with great care. This has been a lot to see, her routine, down to the most vulnerable level. You leave everything exactly as it was.

Shani drops you off at the hospice. She'll be back when it's time to go to the airport. While you're standing in the parking lot feeling sorry for yourself and contemplating a cigarette, your phone vibrates. Aunt Mattie. It's a relief to see an elder calling. You want to be babied.

"Aunt Mattie."

"I wanted to make sure you were okay."

"I'm okay." You should ask if *she's* okay. At times you forget that your mother is also a sister to nine other people. You forget that your pain isn't the only pain just because you feel it so clear.

"I spoke with your mama today. She told me you were out

running errands for her. Getting her stuff handled for when she gets out."

"Yeah."

"You understand the severity of her illness, right?"

"Yes, ma'am." You pause, and she pauses, and then you take the pause to share information with her. "These women had her chart and they were asking me questions. They said the cancer spread to her brain and she's getting confused. Mama didn't say anything about that to me. But it's everywhere, they said."

Aunt Mattie breathes into the phone. You've never known her to cry. "Your mama is in a lot of pain, okay?"

"I know."

"She's holding on for you and your sister."

"Yeah."

"The doctor's already told her they couldn't do anything else. She's holding on for you and you have to be strong enough to tell her that it's okay to let go."

"What do you mean?"

"You have to tell her before you leave that she doesn't have to *fight* anymore. You tell her that you're going to be okay without her."

"But I don't want her to die." You're whining.

"You have to tell her it's okay. That you and Samantha are grown and that she did a good job and y'all are going to be all right. It has to be from you, okay?"

You're leaning against a brick wall, between two bushes and a dumpster, your face covered in tears. She's telling you to tell your mother that it is okay for her to die. She's asking you to give her sister peace. "Okay," you say, "okay."

* * *

Jonathan Frakes:

How does one deal with the inevitability of death? Do we accept it or defy it? Does our belief in survival surpass the natural deterioration of a human body? Can enough prayer summon an unseen God for a miracle? Or are we left to fate? Before we continue, let's take a look back at the stories we've heard tonight.

Our first tale, the school shooting, in which a cheater's guilty gesture ends up saving Sallie's life. Did this all-too-familiar tale of a school shooting actually happen?

Yes. It's *FACT*. Small details may be different, but this is a real event from Sallie's life. The bullet missed her body by mere inches.

Our second story, where the imagined sight of a knife causes Sallie to accidentally hit a child and lose her job. Was this unfortunate occurrence real? Did the boy go on to take the life of a different teacher with the same weapon?

Not this time. *FICTION.* The sad truth, however, is that most of this incident did happen, minus the knife and mystical murder. The only thing that died that day was her career. The boy did try to pick out her hair. She did lose her job and consequently her house over a flippant swat. There was no supernatural savioring in this one, only harsh circumstances.

Lastly, and perhaps the most promising for our current situation, the story of the shadowy male figure that kept Sallie's eyes open until a nurse could notice her low oxygen levels. Was the man an angel sent to save Sallie's life?

This story is true. *FACT.* Sallie almost died that night. Though records show no men working on the floor, Sallie insists a man was with her. A man whose description matches that of her uncle Jack, who had passed a year before. She didn't even know there was a help button, but someone pressed it. That's a fact.

Were you able to catch the lie amongst the miracles? Perhaps there's truth to the saying that real life is stranger than fiction. Are we to believe in angels? That God's divine timing can redirect bullets? Does Sallie have some sort of spiritual mission that spares her life, and if so, is it over? After a brain tumor, ovarian cancer, and breast cancer, will the God she believes in so wholeheartedly restore her health again?

Erika, now on the last day of her visit, must deliver a message that holds a meaning she's not willing to believe. But for the sake of her mother, she must find the words.

She must venture . . . beyond belief. . . .

I'm Jonathan Frakes, good night.

You stop outside the door of room 312. Your mother is sitting in an armchair in an oversized purple sweat shirt and yesterday's gray sweat pants. Her ankles are crossed as she digs through her purse. Sunlight bathes her body, and you take a mental picture of this moment.

A stray tear glides down your cheek, and you swipe it away before making a grand announcement that you're here.

"Hey, baby. You get all my stuff?"

"I did." You hand her the stack of envelopes from the post office and then place her Bible and medication on the little tray with wheels.

"You got my Bible!" She rubs the cover. "This my strength right here. I have to have my word."

She's glowing while she opens her mail. You sit on the edge of her bed and take in everything she does. There's a card from your aunt Vernell. She smiles while she reads whatever her sister wrote and holds up two twenties. "Hey!" She places them inside her Bible so she won't lose them.

Money is meaningless in the grand scheme of things. Most of your life has been about not having enough and trying to get more. It's worthless if you're unable to spend it.

"AARP sends so many damn letters." She flicks through three envelopes before landing on one she likes. "This is from the lawyer about the case!" She opens it quickly. There's only one page, which you know from experience is not enough to deliver good news.

Your mother's bright demeanor goes gloomy. "They threw out the case." She rises to her feet on shaky legs, mad as hell. "After them doctors at Grady spent years using me like a damn lab rat! They gave me experimental pills and treatments like I wasn't even human! Do you know how much suffering I've been through? How many times these doctors made shit worse and then sent me out in the cold because *they needed the space*? Well, guess what, motherfuckers; I need the damn money!"

She's referring to 1998. When they put her out of the hospital right after surgery. She's so angry she starts tearing up, then shrinks down on top of the covers. "They used me for cancer research for twenty years and now they say they done with me. Case closed. No settlement."

The hurt in her eyes is so strong that you finally understand why she's upset. She sued Grady Memorial Hospital for malpractice. It may have been valid and it may have not been, but she was hoping for a settlement and received nothing. It wasn't about her having the money. She knew she probably wasn't going to spend even the two flattened twenties in her Bible. But she wanted to leave her daughters something. She wanted to pay you and Samantha back for the loans, credit card debt, and hotel rooms. She wanted to take care of you after she was gone.

Your mama is lying back onto the plush pillows and weeping. You squeeze in on the twin bed and lay your cheek against her shoulder. "It's okay, Mama."

She's calming down and you pull your cell phone out of your

pocket. Last night you saved her favorite songs to a playlist. "Remember this one, Mama?" The first melodies of a Temptations song begin and your mother can't help but laugh with delight. She sings along to the words; her voice squeaks and cracks.

"*Get ready! Get ready cuz here I come!* We used to dance like this boy." She raises her arms and does her familiar little shimmy. "This was when I was a cute little thing with my big, thick Afro, and my tight jeans." She is grinning now. You're happy for grins and stories. "I remember we snuck off to be on *Teenage Frolics*. We wanted to be on TV. And I don't know how he did it, I think Mattie and Wayne may have ran and told it, but, when we pulled up in the parking lot my daddy was already waiting." Your mama is laughing now. "He say, 'Carol! You got ten seconds to get your *ass* in the car.' He was so mad at me."

The black nurse from yesterday brings in a tray of baked food for your mother to eat and she waves at the two of you scrunched together on the bed. Mama picks at the baked chicken while the nurse tidies up the room. When she leaves, you pull the Cheetos out of the drawer beside the bed and your mama puts her hand in the bag and giggles. The two of you munch on cheese puffs and watch a woman on television talk about how the Lord made her life better. Your mama says there aren't many more channels than this. She doesn't even know what's happening on her soap operas. Her *stories*, as she calls them.

Every time you notice the wall clock beside your mother's bed, your brain starts calculating. Your flight is at 10:30. You should be there by 8:30. You need to leave here at 8:00. It's 6:15 already.

"Look!" Mama frantically turns the volume up with a small remote, gesturing with it toward the television. The news is reporting about the indictment of a superintendent in Georgia who falsified test scores. Twenty-seven out of thirty-five educators in the district turned themselves in to Fulton County Jail, admitting to their involvement. "*That's* the man who wanted me to change them grades for the students! I told you!"

You stare incredulously at the screen, watching a principal be escorted off school property, and then photos of his mug shot. Half the time your mother's ramblings about conniving people go in one ear and out the other. You're never sure if her conspiratorial musings are true or not. The man's mug shot flashes a final time. "Insane," you whisper. They really were playing games at the schoolhouse. *Fact.*

Reeling from the high of a good closed loop, you ask your mother if she'd like to hear a short story that you wrote. She says yes, so you read it out loud from your phone, pausing whenever she interrupts to make comments about the character or to say that you are very talented or to go on a rant about following your dreams.

It amazes her that you can read documents, play music, and watch videos on your phone. The only thing extra she uses hers for is sending lengthy texts to you and your sister that read like emails: *Hello darling, I hope everything is going well.* You show her how Tumblr works, searching "Victor Newman" so she can see all the pictures that populate. She says he looks old but still handsome. The nurse returns with some medication for your mother.

"I don't usually like to take these pills," she says, even though she's been rubbing a painful spot in her lower back for the last hour. "They're too strong. Makes you loopy. I'm not gonna be no drug addict, even in here." She makes a hissing noise and grimaces. "I'm gonna take some tonight, though."

You move to the armchair beside her bed so that she can lie all the way down comfortably. The clock is still ticking behind you. It's 7:10 now. Shani will be here soon. Part of you wants to miss your flight and camp out in this room for as long as your mother is here. The other part of you wants to run.

"I'm getting tired now, Jane."

You pull the covers up to her shoulders. There's a darkness in her face so different from the afternoon light. Her body is betraying her.

She takes your hand. "Do you understand where I am?"

"Yes, Mama."

"I'm in hospice. It's not like a hospital. They aren't treating me here." She is trying to let you know that she understands, and she wants to know you understand too.

"I know, Mama." You sound small.

"I'm in so much pain, baby. I don't know how much longer I can hold out." Her eyes bore into yours so hard that you're scared to look away. You don't want this image to stay with you, but she won't let you see anything else. "Will you be all right?"

Aunt Mattie prepared you for this. You know what she is asking and what you agreed to say, but it doesn't make the words come out any easier. "I'm going to be all right, Mama. Me and Samantha are gonna be okay."

"You always have each other. Remember that, okay? You're sisters."

"Yes, Mama." You remember a Christmas when the three of you had no tree and she got a giant piece of green construction paper and cut it into a tree shape and taped it to the living room wall. She made a game of getting coats on and going outside to pick up leaves and pinecones from the snow-less Georgia ground. When you collected enough, the three of you went inside and taped them to the paper tree, giggling all the while at your shaky creation. It was your favorite Christmas. All the magic had been her. "You did good. We're going to be okay."

"I did good." Your mama's eyes are closed and her head settles down into the pillow. There is the ghost of a smile on her cheek. "I did real good raising my babies."

Her face is peaceful as she drifts to sleep, and you know you've kept your promise. You stand up to find something to busy yourself. Maybe a bit of mess the nurse missed. Your things are strewn about the room and you go about grabbing your notebooks, and puzzle mags, and folding your jacket. Your mother's breathing is haggard, but even as the television in the common area plays soft in the background, a moment of calm, a text from Shani illuminates your cell phone—*I'm outside*. Dread rushes in.

"Mama? I'm about to head out, okay?" You kiss her cheek and then you kiss it one more time. "I love you."

"I love you too, baby. Don't miss your flight. You get home safely, okay." She is talking with her eyes closed, still resting against the pillow. "I would walk you out. But Mama needs to rest right now."

"You rest, Mama." You turn to go, and as soon as you do you feel a violent yank on your wrist. You swivel around and find your mother sitting up in bed, eyes open and magenta colored. She's holding on to you tight.

"I'll see you again, won't I?" She sounds frightened. Your heart aches, and your wrist hurts. "You're gonna come back, right? This isn't the last time I'll see you."

"No, Mama." You swallow down the dry spittle in your mouth. "I'll come back. I'll see you again." You rush forward and hug her tight. She squeezes back with strength you don't recognize, and then it's gone. She sinks back down into the covers and you tuck her in.

"Bye, baby."

"Bye, Mama." You kiss her cheek one more time.

You're crying before you've even left the room. You exit the facility with tearstained cheeks and wet lips because it felt like you were lying. A part of you suspects that you'll never see your mother again. You feel it in your bones. And you know she felt it too.

PART THREE

The Body

Book of Sallie Carol 6:6: If you've got nothing else, have faith.

Let's catch our breath after that, saints. God says come as you are, so walk with me through the church doors and down the aisle between pews. Find yourself a seat. Grab a Bible and a paper fan as the organ begins to play.

In the name of Jesus.

Life sho' can get tough.

What they say? God gives his toughest battles to his what? His strongest soldiers.

I know the trials and tribulations can stack against you so bad the body feels at war, Lord, but we've got to trust and believe that GOD . . . is ALWAYS . . . NEAR. Can I get an amen?

I can't hear you; I said can I get an amen?

How many of y'all grew up with Grandma or Mama or Auntie saying, "Y'all better stop *playing* church"? Well, I'm not here to play today, saints. I'm here to PRAY today; can I get an amen?? I'm here to PRAY!

Can I give my testimony first, saints?

They say a woman carries every egg she will ever have inside her from the moment she's born. That means that like GOD, I've been with my mama every second of her life. HER story is MY story. Her testimony is my testimony. My PROOF OF LIFE; come on, somebody.

I was with her when she was fourteen years old and her appendix burst in the middle of the tobacco fields. And GOD was with her too! Looking over her tiny body lying lifeless in the dirt. It was GOD who sent her brother walking the same way, GOD who had him find her just in time before her life was lost—MY GOD!!! In the name of Jesus—

(Organ swells)

EYE was with her, saints! When one of her own students held a gun to her head, but GOD protected us, can I get an amen? GOD put the bullet in the wall and not the brain, in the name of Jesus. I was with her when my future father revved his engine toward her body and

GOD stood beside her and called the demon inside him off.

(*Organ swells*)

EYE was growing in Mama's belly when the doctors looked at her and said do not have this baby. The brain tumor WILL kill your body. You are GOING to DIE if you have this baby. But MY GOD!!!! What Donnie McClurkin say? "I BELONG HERE!! *It's not wrong, dear.*" My mama said, "I'm having this baby and I . . . Will . . . Live!"

In the name of Jesus, we SURVIVED, and I'm standing here today; can I get an amen?? I can't hear you; I said can I get an amen??

(*Organ swells*)

In 1998, the doctors said Mama had two years to live. But what did GOD SAY?

Not one!

(*Organ*)

Not two!

(*Organ*)

Not three!

(Organ)

She lived to see TEN MORE YEARS with air in her lungs; CAN I GET AN AMEN!!!!!!!!!!

(Organ swells)

Something about the name Jesus. Somebody pass me a handkerchief. I'm SWEATIN' in the GLORY OF GOD!!!! In 2006, the doctors said the cancer's back. The doctors said Mama had MONTHS to live. *BUT WHAT DID GOD SAY???*

The years start coming and they don't stop coming, saints!

2013! AND SHE'S STILL HERE! IN THE NAME OF JESUS!

CAN I GET AN AMEN!

I ask the congregation, When have we EVER taken a MORTAL'S words over what GOD can do? My God makes a way out of no way. My God can turn water to wine, can stretch two fish to feed five thousand! My God performs miracles!

I need y'all to pray with me today. We need to ask God won't He do it just one more time, in the name of Jesus. I need y'all to bow your heads with me please, don't close your eyes, keep reading, but pray with me.

All we have left is faith. We can save her life, right here and right now. That's the only option, saints; I need you to pray.

Father God, in the name of Jesus, do you remember when I was nine and we lived in that shack, and Mama sent me and my sister to the park to play? And when we came back she was crying on the bed and asked us to come sit with her. And when we were beside her she opened her balled fist to reveal a handful of pills and she admitted that she was gonna kill herself while we were outside. But she couldn't bear the thought of us finding her body, or of leaving her baby girls all alone in the world. Do you remember that, Jesus? How she wanted to live. She wanted to live for us, Father God. Can you keep her alive for us now?

Because please, Father, don't you remember when I came home from college after we lost the house? And we had to stay in that raggedy apartment. And one night Mama burst into my room crying and screaming and saying she was really going to do it, and threw the whole bottle of pills into her mouth. Do you remember how I had to wrestle her to the ground, Father God? How I had to force her mouth open and take the pills out myself while she cried? How I had to lay her down in her bed and rub her back until she fell asleep? Do you remember all the burdens I had to bear, Father God? Can you please just save her? For me? Haven't I been through enough?

Remember when she had an acid reflux attack so bad that she collapsed on the floor of my bedroom while asking for help, and then lay lifeless while I sat beside her whispering, *Mama, Mama, Mama, Mama*? I didn't know what to do then. I sat staring until you brought her back, oh God; with one big cough and a gasp for air you brought her back. I want to believe you can save her again. I want to believe so bad, oh God.

When you been fighting demons for so long, all you want is the comfort of your mother's hug at the end of the day. I think now of the television program *Buffy the Vampire Slayer*. She was the *protector* of her town. She fought *supernatural* forces piled against her while she did her *homework*. And yet even a girl as powerful as the chosen one could be emotionally *DESTROYED*, when the most natural of causes left her mother's body sprawled across the living room couch. Her trauma created a visualization of my greatest fear.

Oh, saints, if she can't bear the pain how will I? Buffy went on to sacrifice her own life, for her sister, for the world, and maybe even for an end to her own struggles. I'm reminded of her friends, who performed *black magic* to resurrect her body and renew her soul! But by the next season, Buffy cries out, "I think I was in heaven," describes *no pain, no fear, no doubt*, before they brought her back to keep fighting with them. Am I no better now, Lord? If our strongest savior can wish for death, does that make my prayer selfish? Even Christ on the cross prayed for an end to his suffering.

Saints, are you still with me? Can we pray together? For a will, for a way, for a miracle? The Clark Sisters say, "Is my living in vain? Is my praying in vain?" Am I wasting my time, Lord? Please pray with me, saints, in the name of Jesus. Can you help us please, Father God? Father, God! Two things I've never seen in my life. A Father. A God. But I have to have faith.

She'll live. She'll live. She WILL live.

In the name of Jesus.

We pray,

Amen.

November

The end of October was for pretending life was normal. Not call-ing Mommy was average young adult behavior. You focused on making it official with Chris, a coworker turned friend, turned something more. Another thing that normal people do. You made sure it played out like a romance movie. Dramatically ending the casual fling when he couldn't articulate his feelings. Keeping tabs on him through mutuals. Getting word back that he felt remorse and missed you. Showing up sexy with your roommate at a party at his house. You loved when he grabbed your arm, demanded a moment alone, told you he was happy to see you.

The two of you became boyfriend-girlfriend at 2:00 am on his beer-stained couch; you noted the date, *October 18*. Desperate for a new milestone, a different counter, something positive for the month. You take your first couple's selfie on your cell phone, making sure to smize, making sure not to think of your mother flipping through her Bible on a hospice bed, three states away. This one is a happy day. No tragedies.

Any day could be the day it happens. You don't know when it's coming or how badly it will hurt. You don't know who will be the one to tell you or how they will say it. Your sister, who you used to call every day, now gets a once-weekly text. Enough to say you've spoken. You're both grieving privately. Anticipating the loss of two different versions of the same woman. She wasn't a mom the same way twice. One isn't sure how to comfort the other.

For Samantha, Mama was a married woman, one who coached cheerleading *and* basketball at the high school where she taught. A woman scorned, a woman educated, a woman sickly. Samantha was a daddy's girl without a father; then a big sister to the baby. Her mama downgraded from a house, changed cities, tried, and failed. Her mama got credit cards in her daughter's name, had her changing high schools with every new apartment or employer, made her hand over paychecks from her part-time job to help with the bills. Her mama had strict rules. Your mama did not.

Your mama was a single parent, one who taught school when she could and offered counseling on the weekends. She was a woman scorned, a woman educated, a woman sickly, several times over. And a woman jailed. You were a mama's girl who had to stay with her auntie. Your mama downgraded from apartments to hotels, changed towns, had you changing elementary schools with every new job, lost your toys in evictions. When you were in high school she told you not to work, to be a child, but in college you were wiring her half your paychecks.

Same, same, but different. The good parts were mostly similar. Mama's humor. Her playfulness. Her everlasting support. You were each other's witness to bad parts but digested them differently. Samantha kept a safe distance, physically and emotionally. You went a distance but didn't keep it. Mama loved you both to death.

To death.

You'll call Samantha later. She has Damon now, a college best friendship that turned into love. You have Chris. It's normal sister distance when you both start dating, nothing more. Your boyfriend threw a Halloween party and you thought to yourself, *Please don't die today. Let me have fun for one night.* You think this on a lot of days. When you meet his friends, you picture yourself ahistorical. They don't know where you've been, and you can tell them where you're going. Most of them hail from the suburbs of Chicago. They go home for dinner on Sundays after partying like they have no parents on Saturday, their family tree only half an hour away. The world seems to have gone easy on them. You pretend yours has too.

For Halloween you're dressed as Sister Mary Clarence from *Sister Act*. Chris wears a Mordecai hat from *Regular Show*. He's a cartoon and you're a shenanigan in hiding. There's a couple dressed as Neo and Trinity from *The Matrix* and the image burrows inside your mind. Next year the two of you will be cohesive. This year you lay low. The party is a success. Everyone leaves drunk and happy. Your phone never rang, though Samantha texts a photo of her Wednesday Addams costume.

You blink awake in Chris' small bed. November's sunshine lies across your face through the curtainless windows. Time is an insidious countdown. Aunt Mattie told you Mama had two months left three months ago. Unease fills your stomach. You should call her.

You should.

The Spirit

The dorm room era was over. Sophomore year in the expensive housing that looked like townhomes had drained my refund checks. Brittani and I shared the master bedroom on the second floor with a private bathroom and big tub, but I spent both semesters working as a desk receptionist in the dorms for my spending money. Which was fine by me, less time spent in the room watching Brittani prepare for acting challenges from the theater school I'd been kicked out of. My schoolwork now consisted of writing fiction starring cynical women with no faith. College was rather dull without the tease of fame.

While I was writing stories, Mama was packing our house into a U-Haul and quietly moving into an apartment. I was devastated. The house had come to represent the end of our struggle era, a healthy distance from life in hotels. I couldn't decipher over the phone if she'd been evicted or made the decision herself, and in either scenario it made me sad to picture a woman whose cancer had just gone into remission packing up a three-bedroom house alone.

When I came home for spring break, my suspicions were confirmed. Our lives had been downgraded to a run-down and outdated apartment complex near South DeKalb Mall. It was still a three-bedroom with a second level, but the stairs had a metal railing like we were outside, and it was weird seeing my things stuffed into a room I didn't recognize. It took everything in me to smile and say it wasn't bad. On top of everything else, her boyfriend, Henry, had fallen ill; he needed oxygen tanks and his legs and feet were often swollen. After years of being the sickly one, she was sure to remain by his side, but the burden was definitely showing.

By Thanksgiving break he had passed away. Mama took it tough, especially after she spent months washing his feet like the woman in the Bible had done for Jesus. She squeezed the yellow-gray puss out of the boils on his legs and wiped up the dampness with a warm towel. She helped him walk up the stairs to his room. She'd visited him multiple times a week at the VA hospital. She'd been part of his life. Yet his daughter from a previous marriage wouldn't let Mama see him after his death and had the body flown to Michigan. She was devastated.

When I got to the apartment the power bill hadn't even been paid. We spent Thanksgiving at the movie theater in the mall, charging our phones against the wall. This was the visit where she threw my bedroom door open and threatened to take the pills. I felt for her so heavy, but I also couldn't bear to visit again.

The next summer, heading into junior year, it was my turn to choose where we lived while Logan spent the months back home in Virginia. Her father would cosign for us and pay the down payment, so half the battle was already won. She had originally chosen a basement apartment, just twenty minutes west of campus. It had cement walls painted different colors in each room, a display shelf of doll heads nailed to the wall, and a weird lingering vibe from the alcoholic artist who stayed there previously. The place was fine until it flooded. We'd waded through the water with Logan's two black cats until sea levels shrank, but the smell and the mold never quite waned.

When I got a big-girl apartment there would be no plotting and scheming for rent like Mama. The thought terrified me. Her life was a soap opera I'd been trapped in for too long. No sexy subplots but lots of jaw-dropping twists, oscillating between *The Bold and the Beautiful* and *The Young and the Restless*. I would break the pattern. Make good decisions. Keep a steady job. Be a normal person. The drive for stability felt more important than college to me. Preparing for the life that came after.

Mama may have loosely named me after edgy Erica Kane from *All My Children*, but I wanted to be a fixer. On *Scandal*, Olivia Pope was a gladiator in a suit. A woman who made her own name despite a shadowy father. A woman with know-how and connections, who solved problems for world leaders and made nasty history disappear, including her own. She'd hiss, "It's handled," into her cell phone before the click of a camera shifted scenes.

camera shutter clicks

The apartment was in a Polish neighborhood within Avondale. I'd found the place on Craigslist after a half-hour search. A Realtor with an Eastern European accent and dirty-blonde bob had me follow her up a dingy staircase. On the first floor, a door on the left creaked open as we headed toward the next set of stairs. An older woman in an ankle-length housedress started squawking, "Krystina! Sufit wciąż przecieka! Kiedy przyjdą?"

My eyebrows raised. I loved ghetto behavior in other cultures.

"Dzień dobry, Maria," Krystina answered in a singsong voice. "Przyjdą wkrótce!" I could tell she was bullshitting the lady with pleasantries because the lady responded with a frown and slammed her front door closed. We kept climbing up the steps and stopped on the next floor.

"Apartment Three. Very good deal," Krystina said, getting back to business. The unit was wood paneled, floor to ceiling. Tackily so. To the right, sunlight poured into a wide space through a three-panel window. To the left, a long hallway led to a bedroom at the first door, a bathroom at the second, then a living room connected to a kitchen with linoleum floors. Outdated. Straight out of the seventies in design. It charmed the hell out of me.

"That's the master bedroom." Krystina gestured toward the large space to my right, with the gorgeous windows and their promising sun rays. My eyes lit up. Logan said I could have the big bedroom this time. At the previous place, my room was an office attached to Logan's room with a tapestry covering the glass door for privacy.

"Seven hundred dollars a month, this one," Krystina said, looking down at her flip phone like she wasn't showing me a place outside my price range. Logan said the max was $650. Any higher and we might struggle. I could make the right decision or I could make a good decision. I could have the master. What was $50? Wasn't I worth it? With the gusto of Mama swiping a credit card in one of her daughter's names, I nodded vigorously, *We'll take it.*

camera shutter clicks

A year and a half passed easy. Since I still had to make up for two semesters wasted on theater school credits, Logan graduated first.

She decided to head toward a new life in Paris, leaving behind three black cats for me to raise as a single black mother. Familiar narrative, but I could handle it. I held it down with a job at Target. Kept doing my English major studies even though I wasn't sure where that story line was taking me. I hung tight to the apartment, knowing that without Logan's father to cosign, my name alone wouldn't secure more housing.

I revisited Craigslist to find another white woman. I didn't mention the cats or the hamster I adopted in a fit of needing control. She didn't tell me she was a flight risk, passing through on her way out of Wisconsin. A month later, she was gone, crept out in the middle of the night like Mama avoiding past due rent. She left behind a single box full of VHS tapes. This was fine. My priorities were graduating from college and maintaining this apartment. The future would work itself out if I could just manage these two things.

A boy I worked at Target with needed a place to stay. I had never been that close to a man before, but I knew he had a check coming in and that was enough for me. I tried to give him relief by teaching him some of Mama's tricks: ***Book of Sallie Carol 2:7: The money isn't due, due until the fifth of the month. Landlords can't legally evict a nonpaying tenant until the third month.*** Problem is, you can't tell things like that to a dummy little boy. He immediately stopped paying rent on time, and then at all. Surprise, surprise, a black man had failed me again.

I had to evict him before he got me evicted. If I wanted to avoid house hopping like Mama I'd have to squat in this apartment with my expired lease like nobody's business. I dead-bolted the door. He climbed through the window, voice first, spewing all sorts of "dumb fucking bitchs" while he put his things in a trash bag. Worst was that I had company over—a friend from Tumblr I was meeting in real life for the first time. Embarrassing. My former roommate left behind nine hundred dollars of past due rent debt.

Being an adult was tougher than I anticipated. I was experiencing the evil forces, plots, and people that Mama so often referenced. What Olivia Pope failed to realize, while she was desperately trying to be the opposite of her villainous father, is that by being someone who's there, someone who helps those around her instead of hurts, she was actually exactly like him: headstrong, calculating, a lil crazy if the mission called for it. She couldn't outrun her genealogy. It made her who she was. Turns out I wasn't nothing but Sallie Carol in box braids, hustling for rent while dreaming of superstardom.

camera shutter clicks

"Is this Erika Simpson?" The voice on the other end of the phone waited patiently for my response. The area code of her phone number was 404, so the call was from Atlanta.

"Yes." My tone was even, revealing no emotion. It was 7:00 pm, but with the time difference between Chicago and Atlanta this could still be a bill collector after a minimum payment on the credit card Mama ran up in my name or the ten-thousand-dollar personal loan that we were supposed to start paying on after my freshman year of college. Three years later, it all added up to nearly fifty thousand with interest.

The woman continued in a calm, measured voice, "I'm calling from Fulton County Jail. We have your mother in a holding cell until she's moved tomorrow morning. You can see the charges online in twenty-four hours."

"Jail! What did she do?" My unbothered tone had vanished, replaced with a desperation for information.

"You can check the charges online in twenty-four hours."

Her delivery revealed nothing. I tried not to let it infantilize me. Surely she could be reasoned with. "I'm in Chicago, ma'am. And her brothers and sisters are in North Carolina. No one can come right away. I just need to know what happened."

"You can check the charges online in twenty-four hours."

Then why the fuck even call? I wanted to say, but I hung up in her face instead. I grabbed my laptop and googled "Fulton County Jail" furiously. *What did she do?* Growing up in Decatur, Georgia, I heard a lot of stories about police and police chases and unjust nights spent in jail from guys at school and friends' boyfriends and some of our parents if we were being honest with each other during sleepovers. I'd already sat in the police department while Mama was being processed when I was eight years old. I had no information then and none now. I spent the rest of the night in unease. I called my sister to fill her in on the latest unfortunate happenings with Mama, then tried to wait the twenty-four hours patiently.

The next day, a mug shot and the charges were indeed up online via an inmate search. According to the report, the sheriff was sent to evict her from the apartment that was already a downgrade from the house. She refused to leave, so they dragged her from the premises by force. She went into what they listed as a "hyper-religious fit" and swung her cane around attempting to hit as many people as possible before throwing herself on the ground and shouting out to God.

I read each sentence with wide eyes. Mama was intelligent. She had several degrees in various fields. She wasn't . . . Maybe there was a strategy to this. Maybe she had swung her cane to be bad enough to go to jail. Then she'd have three meals and a bed at least. It was better than the streets. There was still one more sentence of the report to read.

Inmate transferred to mental facility.

I read the sentence again, trying to comprehend it. My phone rang. Another call from an Atlanta area code. I took a deep breath and answered.

A woman with a drippy sweet voice said she was calling from Grady Memorial Hospital. I couldn't piece together fast enough if it related to the sentence I just read. She said she had a few questions concerning Mama.

"So your mother had what we call a *hyper-religious outburst* during her eviction. And we wanted to ask some questions about her mental history. Has she always displayed behaviors like this?"

My eyesight blurred. Mama said never, ever tell your business to anyone, especially not people from institutions, people who had the power to break up your family. ***Conceal what's real, Book of Sallie Carol 2:6.***

This was serious. Far beyond what I was prepared to deal with, and there was too much to process quickly. Mama had been evicted. The last place I lived with her was now an empty home, which meant our things were piled like trash in the parking lot. I tried not to mentally review a checklist of items I'd taken with me versus ones that were with Mama. My birth certificate was safe, my senior yearbook too. My books from growing up, gone. High school diploma, gone. The binder full of stories and self-insert *Angel* fan fiction I'd written all throughout high school, gone. This wasn't the time to give myself a stomachache with loss, though.

They'd taken Mama to jail. And whether it was intentional or not, part of some grand backup plan her Gemini brain had concocted on the spot, the gambit had failed. Her faith in God during a violent emotional outburst had been too much and they had transferred her to the loony bin. I wasn't sure if it was its own building or a floor within Grady, but this was real life.

What was I supposed to tell a professional yet sincere-sounding woman who needed information to diagnose my mother correctly? I wished I could phone a friend like on *Who Wants to Be a Millionaire?* and call my sister. Tell her we have thirty seconds to decide if we're airing out every irrational decision our mother has made throughout our lives or revealing nothing. The woman waited for an answer in expectant silence.

I took a deep breath and did the only thing that felt natural. I told the truth. Through the years, Mama had been prone to paranoia. It started around the first time she lost her teaching job. She started feeling like the world was against her. The school system and the government. The people at the post office were responsible for losing her mail. Her sister Linda was conspiring with her doctors to give her the wrong medicine. All of these were things that she believed wholeheartedly. My sister and I stopped trying to point out flaws in her thought process and instead resigned ourselves to half listening and fractionally agreeing. It had been like this for so long that we did not consider she might be mentally ill.

My mother strongly disliked being called crazy. It felt horrible to speak against Mama, but the woman on the phone promised everything would stay between us. When I finally got to call my sister, I discovered she had done the same.

Nothing happened for two whole days. I went to work at Target, came home, drank two-dollar bottles of wine. And then my phone rang again. Another 404 number. I braced myself.

"Jane?"

"Mama!" I proclaimed, relieved to hear her voice, sounding even and calm.

"What an ordeal I've been through, baby. They put me out of the apartment. I may have acted up too much. I was just so upset. But I'll apply to teach more DUI classes. Figure out where to go from here."

She didn't sound like they had her locked in a padded room, arms bound at her sides in a straitjacket.

"They make me take pills while I'm here." She paused for a moment. "They say I'm bipolar. I don't know. We'll see how it goes."

The information was given calmly. I nodded like she could hear it. Whimpered that everything's okay. We talked a little more. She didn't mention any game playing from the staff. She didn't ask if anyone called me for personal information about her past. I didn't bring it up. We exchanged "I love yous" and I hung up. My brain was racing. She sounded different than before. Like her fight was missing, or maybe her edge. She would call Samantha, and then we could debrief together. What if she just needed medication? All these years? What if there was a reality where she had an early diagnosis, thought more clearly, made less risky choices? Where would we all be?

It was another two days before my phone rang again. This time, the caller ID showed Mama's actual cell phone number. "Mama?"

Her tone was different. "I'm out. Those damn people try to

pump me with pills until I don't know who the hell I am. I'm a child of *God*; that's who I am!" Wind whisked in her background like she was walking fast. "They not about to put me in a loony bin and throw away the key! Invalidate my intelligence! Nawl! I ain't taking them damn pills. I got work to do."

I held the phone up to my ear. Brow furrowed. Stomach uneasy. Mama was back. That was my realest reaction to what she was saying. Mama's back and out on the streets again. No telling what the plan was. Before I could comment on the pills or the place, Mama added something else.

"They gave me my paperwork too. I saw everything you and your prissy-ass sister said about me to the doctors." *Oh god.* "Don't you worry about me, Miss Erika. No more. Me and my paranoia will be just fine."

The wind cut out, as did her impassioned voice. She'd hung up. I'd never been on the wrong side of Mama's trust. Always her baby, her confidant, the last person standing beside her. I'd broken one of her commandments.

My stomach settled on a violent ache.

camera shutter clicks

She was coming: Mama. I used one of my Target checks to fly her out to visit me in the big city. She was gonna see how I lived in my Polish neighborhood with its sausage shops and kooky characters. We sat on the phone as she went through the airport. I warned her that she could only have one carry-on and one checked bag, but she was bringing three bags anyway. She said she needed everything she was bringing, and I knew it wasn't shoes and dresses but her business notes, her Bible, her books, and her pile of medications.

What was unspoken was that she couldn't leave anything behind in a hotel room. Even if the items made the straps of her book bag dig into her shoulders. Weight she shouldn't be carrying on her fragile body.

"Miss, please. I'm going to see my baby up in Chicago. I had a brain tumor when she was born. I'm a cancer survivor. See?" She was probably wearing the pink college-themed breast cancer T-shirt that she stole the second I brought it home two years ago. Her voice quivered with tears, but I only shook my head on the other side of the receiver. She was using her story to get her way.

"Okay, Ms. Simpson, it's all right. Calm down. I can give you the second bag as a courtesy, but I can't apply it for the way back."

I could hear Mama smile. "Thank you, ma'am. Thank you. Don't worry, we'll get it back. God will make a way. God bless you." The smallest smile hit the corner of my mouth. This lady. So stubborn and still got her way. "See, Jane?" she said. "My God will work it out."

"Mm-hm. Well, I will see you in three or four hours I guess." She'd flown before, but I was still so excited to give her a trip. The winter chill of Chicago did make me anxious for her immune system. She was always strong in spirit, but what if she got sick or slipped on a spot of black ice?

It felt so adult to be the one waiting at the airport. We took selfies on the train after, both grinning big at reuniting. Mama had her cane with her, a sight I'd grown more used to, and the third leg eased my nervousness about the ice. We dropped off her three bags at my apartment, and Mama made the downturned yet impressed smile at my humble wooden home. It warmed me from head to toe and reminded me that her thin jacket wasn't enough for Chicago's winter, so we headed to the thrift store before the sun set.

I took her to Unique on Elston Avenue, my favorite location. Logan put me onto thrifting, showed me how to get four shirts and a pair of pants for seven dollars, and it changed my life. I'd gone from wearing my high school wardrobe with free college T-shirts mixed in to wearing patterns, striped leggings, and vests. I showed Mama how good-quality winter coats were only ten dollars, and half off on Mondays if they had the right-color ticket attached.

"Good job, Jane," she said, flipping through different-style coats. Pleather, fur lined, trench, bomber. My chest swelled as she tried one on. I offered to buy it for her. I was doing all right. Giving back. Showing Mama a new city.

Back at the apartment, I caught her up on all the assorted dramas of the neighbors within the building: "The old lady downstairs has two live-in boyfriends, but we only ever see one. Her son broke the glass on the door downstairs when his baby mama locked him out. The girl upstairs gets endless packages for her car, but her car's still raggedy, so something's suspicious there...." Mama raised her eyebrows with intrigue. I taught her how to tell my black cats apart: "Oscar has a thin, long tail and hides in the closet all day. Red is the man of the house, he's always out." I told her I had to go to work in the morning, but I'd be back by 3:30. "If you go down to the Burger King, don't forget the key."

The next day, we watched a little television and talked over it. While she changed into her silk nightgown, she showed me how much weight she'd lost, putting up strongman arms while posing in her white grandma undies. I giggled as I keeled into the bedsheets and snapped a pic with my cell phone. "What you take? Don't you show nobody!" She scowled. Then, "Let me see!" excitedly. We didn't talk too much about where she was living, but about the games people were playing, from the post office to the government.

On our last full day together, Mama scrubbed the carpet on the cat tree with a rag, the lightest glistening of sweat at her brow.

"What are you doing, Mama?" I asked, bemused.

"Taking care of your cats." She stuck her tongue out at me. "This thang was just as dirty, covered in fur, and smelling like piss."

"That's my bath rag, Mama!" I whined. Half playfully, half kinda mad for real. She said I should have cleaned faster then, and I couldn't argue with that. We went to see The Bean in Millennium Park, took goofy pictures of our bendy reflections. Mama looked sharp and warm in the new black trench coat. We were happy.

That night, Mama and I got to arguing about something irrelevant. Coldly, meanly, I said she sounded crazy. She turned as red as a black person can get and stormed off into my bedroom, slamming the door and locking it. She was boiling mad, screaming at the top of her lungs that she was *NOT crazy!* My stomach ached with regret. I tap-tapped on the door with the palms of my hands, begging her to forgive me, afraid she would make herself faint from this emotional outburst, scared she'd do something dangerous to herself. She shouted until the words became a prayer, loud and long and meant for me to hear every word, and only after she said amen did she open the door for me again. I apologized with tears in my eyes. We hugged; we ate; we watched television, Mama talking over it.

Sending her back to Georgia made me nauseated. We couldn't

say she was going back home because there wasn't much home down there, what with her hotel hopping. I should have offered for her to stay with me. I had a roommate, but my room was big. Mama and I could share the bed. Maybe I was a selfish person. I couldn't handle everything.

We rode to the airport departure more soberly than from the arrival. Squeezing our gloved hands together, taking turns each letting her beanie head rest on the other's shoulders.

At the airport, Mama explained breathlessly to the employee working in baggage that she couldn't afford a second checked bag but couldn't leave it. Her medicines, her research, she explained. The woman showed kindness. Mama smirked back at me, but we were both a lil sad. It had been a nice trip. We hugged tight. I waved her off and stood watching her book bag and cane until she disappeared into the security line.

camera shutter clicks

For the last two months of college, I had no roommate outside of the cats. It was kismet in that I had a spare room for my sister and Mama to occupy for the big graduation visit, but difficult on my wallet.

In school, I had finally embraced narrative creation. I liked writing fiction because my facts were too depressing and there was no happy ending for Mama yet. I wrote stories about bisexual artists, snarky sisters, and introspective women grappling with marriage and kids as their fate. Before Samantha graduated, she had a piece published in her school's literary magazine, the *Kenyon Review*, and I longed to be able to say the same. My creepy piece where a girl fantasizes about kidnapping her sister's baby didn't get published, so I decided I had failed overall. Where was my life leading? Mama was stuck still struggling and I had no forward motion to stardom. But I was graduating nonetheless. The quiet part of my brain was thankful Mama lived to see it.

It had been a year since Mama's last visit. I was proud. Not just of the degree, but that I'd manage to maintain the apartment. Proved I could create stability for myself. Samantha would be flying in from Greensboro too. Mama and Samantha's relationship was a bit strained, so as excited as I was at the thought of being together again, I also prayed for a visit with no arguments.

Mama came first, leaning on her cane and looking proud as hell of me. Education was the most important thing to Mama, and her second daughter had earned a degree. We sway-hugged in the airport. She marveled at summertime Chi. So different from the bone-rattling chill she'd experienced before.

Samantha arrived the next day, and we all looked at each other with sly grins, our old dynamic settling in. Mama demanded pictures of us together on my digital camera. Samantha rolled her eyes, while I bounced like a baby. For brunch, Samantha treated us to a diner off the Belmont Red Line. Mama scoffed at twelve-dollar pancakes, and I asked what our budget was. Samantha told us to just pick something and eat, shaking her head like we were silly, telling us not to worry about the prices for once.

Mama smiled, simultaneously a proud mama and a sweet baby. Samantha, almost thirty, felt sturdier than us with her adjunct teaching money and her responsible attitude, much less concerned with the distant big dream like Mama and me, and more with the day-to-day practicals.

The night before graduation, we upset Mama. Nothing heavy,

just family fussing. While Samantha and I lay on my bed in the dark, Mama paced the room, praying loudly, half cursing us out and half blessing our heads. We said nothing. Flashbacked to the days of our youth, eyes closed, huddled close, listening to her pray out to God for help. She joined us after she calmed. Whispering, "Amen, amen, amen," as she slid beneath the sheets.

We took the bus to graduation. I wore my cap and gown, and Mama made us pose together for pictures at the bus stop and again outside the stadium. "Why do I have to be in them?" Samantha griped, to which Mama snapped that she wanted pictures of us together, *dammit!* And we posed some more. I walked the stage and got my English degree. It was finally handled. We jammed into a compact car with my friend Azalea's family to get back home, thighs and knees all mushed together.

The next day we went to Navy Pier. When Shani worked at Six Flags in high school, I went all the time for free. But I'd never gone to an amusement park with Mama, since we were usually on a survival budget. Samantha got us little blue ticket stubs good for two main attractions.

We rode the Wave Swinger ride first. Mama left her cane in the purse area. It was a marvel just to see her face light up beneath the warm twinkle of the ride, her open-mouth smile while we went steadily higher, picking up wind, soaring in a circle through the air above the world. Her laugh, a gift.

We rode the Ferris wheel next. "Chicago!" I exclaimed as our buggy swayed at the top of the circle. "Ain't she beautiful?"

Mama nodded, head rested atop her hands on her cane. "We could take over this whole city," she said, eyes glowing with all the ways she could help people and make money in a place like this.

Samantha shook her head, amused. "We don't have to take it over, you know? We can just enjoy it."

Mama let that sink in, then laughed, lifting her head from the cane and leaning back into the seat. "I guess that's right, huh? We can enjoy it."

And we did.

`*camera shutter clicks*`

November

It's Thanksgiving. You attempt to write in your journal but aren't sure what to say. Everything feels like a version of a sob story that you've read before, and every time you try to talk genuinely, your eyes water.

You flinch when the phone rings.

Maybe it's your aunt Mattie. You picture her leaning in the doorway, once again offering information. She'll tell you that your mother has stopped breathing. She'll tell you that she went peacefully in her sleep.

Maybe it's your sister. You know it'll be her. "Hey, Sister," she'll say, fishing around in the open. "Where are you? Are you with anyone?" Then she'll catch you, say something beautiful, like *She's gone now.* She's a writer; she wouldn't just say *she died.*

Technically Mama beat the allegations again. She was still here and the doctors only guaranteed two months. It's been three weeks since you saw her. You know if someone calls and leaves a voicemail that everything's okay. If they don't, you assume she's gone. Some information is too sensitive to record. You haven't written a sentence in your journal. Pens down. You send a text.

Happy Thanksgiving, Sister.

Thank you, Sister, she replies. *I'm making Tofurky for Damon.* You grin at her boyfriend's willingness to eat her vegetarian meals. Maybe you both have keepers.

She is being normal today and you are not. You should go to the living room with your boyfriend and your roommate, Shawn, the person you could thank for suggesting you give Chris a chance. The three of you all met working at Target and somehow became a unit, a family of sorts. You should offer to cook so everyone can do something with their mouths besides smoke.

You should call your mother, but you are afraid to hear the fatigue in her voice. You don't want to picture her in that place, in that room, don't want to think about her being alone on Thanksgiving or the piece of turkey the black nurse will bring in. Don't want to feel guilty for not being there.

You make your way into the living room. Chris and Shawn are on the couch passing a joint between them. The television's playing *America's Next Top Model* reruns. They look up at you expectantly.

"Let's cook." You take the joint from your boyfriend's fingers and inhale from it deeply. Shawn suggests ordering Chinese to save trouble and you shake your head no. "We have to cook." You look back and forth between them. "We should."

Chris nods. "We should, baby."

You head toward the kitchen. It will be nice to create a sense of family. The three of you who chose to leave your mothers in other states can now boast about how family is what you make it while taking hits off a bong.

You place a pot on top of the stove and choose to ignore the thick film of grease and crumbs. Aunt Mattie makes gooey mac and cheese on the stovetop and hot biscuits from scratch. You know the ingredients but can't mimic the taste or texture. You're going to try for Thanksgiving. Fail happily. Cook as mediocre as your mother.

There's no whole turkey, which you're grateful for because you wouldn't know how to make it. Instead, you'll prepare ready-to-eat turkey wings that you bought on sale at Aldi's last week. You aren't sure if you should throw them in the oven as is or attempt to sprinkle random spices on first.

You never learned how to work a kitchen because your mama didn't know. She made things like whole-wheat spaghetti noodles with tuna and mixed vegetables. You laugh at the memory. She served it to you with a slice of white bread, then raved about her new decision to eat healthy. You were happy she was happy, but you were also very hungry that night.

What else did your mother make? You remember her biscuits with the burnt bottoms, snack foods like oatmeal crème pies, honeybuns, and pretzels. You can't recall what she made on the days when you had a working stove in a place caught up on the rent. There was tilapia, for sure. The water in the pot starts boiling, and you add some macaroni in without measuring. You call for Chris to set up a board game. It'll be nice to have something to do. Mama used to make board games so fun. She'd do full detective monologues over a game of Clue, changing voices between Professor Plum and Miss Scarlett, making up elaborate scenes about affairs and candlestick killings until you were out of breath laughing. You stir the noodles and check on the turkey wings.

Meatloaf! She made meatloaf with the ketchup sauce on top. You should call her, for real. You should let her know you're thinking of her. For now, you drain the noodles and search for something to shred a block of cheese with.

It's nighttime. You're lying naked in bed beside Chris. After dinner and board games and ice cream, you-all drifted off into a bedroom to lie horizontal. Your food digested while the two of you lie talking. In the back of your head, you kept calculating what time it was in Georgia as compared to here. She's an hour ahead. You still have time to call. It is nine o'clock and ten o'clock in Georgia and you can't wait any longer if you're going to do a Thanksgiving phone call. Chris lies still with his back to you, asleep. You reach for your phone.

You listen to the rings and bite your nails, let your gaze drift out the window. It is gloomy outside, and the streetlights make the parked cars look sinister.

"Hello?" Your mother sounds as if she either has just woken up or is drifting off to sleep.

"Hi, Mama," you whisper into the receiver, and wait. You don't know what else to say. There are no positive things to add. *I love you. I miss you. You're dying. What did we eat for dinner all those years?* Instead, you hold the phone and bite your nails and stare at the streetlamps outside like an idiot. You say nothing. And she says nothing. Perhaps she is also thinking of all the things she should say: *I miss you. I love you. I'm in pain. I wish we could've all had dinner together today.*

Instead, she says, "Mama's not feeling too good right now, baby. I'm gonna rest. Okay? I'll call you back when I feel a little better."

You notice now, of all moments, that your mother speaks in

third person a lot. Maybe that way it feels like her life is happening to someone else. You understand this. "Okay."

"All right, baby."

With that she is gone. You're still holding the phone to your face. You didn't say, *I love you.* That's important these days. To say "I love you" as often as possible. So she remembers. So she knows it's true even though you chose to be far away.

You place the phone down on the windowsill and curl your body around Chris. He's warm and healthy and alive. You begin to cry against his back, and he instinctively turns to hold you. He doesn't know what's wrong and you can't bear to tell him. Instead, you close your eyes tight, clear your mind, try to let sleep take you instead of the preemptive grief. You re-create the phone call in your head, give yourself a memory you can handle:

                         ERIKA
Hello? Mama?

                         MAMA
Hey, baby!

                         ERIKA
Happy Thanksgiving! I wish I was there
with you so much, much, much. What did
they feed you?

                         MAMA
Girl, they gone bring in a tray of
damn deli meat.

                         ERIKA
             (cackles)

MAMA

Talking 'bout some
HappyThanksgivingMs.Simpson like they
speaking to a baby, then hand me the
thinnest lil ol' piece of meat and a
lump of mashed potatoes that look like
Play-Doh.

ERIKA

Was there gravy at least??

MAMA

Trust it if you want to. [Both laugh.]
I ain't too hungry no way.

ERIKA
        (beat)
Well, you wouldn't have been any
better with me. I call myself buying
some premade turkey wings.

MAMA

Wings sound good.

ERIKA

If I knew how to cook 'em!

[Both laugh.]

MAMA

It ain't nothing but putting it in the
oven, Jane. Even I can do that.

ERIKA

Well, it came out just as dry. That
gravy saved my life.

MAMA

And who you cooking for, you still
dating the white boy?

ERIKA

(whispers)

I am still dating the white boy.

MAMA

What? He there now? Lordddd.

ERIKA

(laughs into the phone)

MAMA

That's all right, baby; you go on. I'm
feeling tired now.

ERIKA

I love you, Mama. I miss you.

MAMA

I love you too, baby. And ain't no
missin' me; I ain't going nowhere.

ERIKA

I'll call you tomorrow?

MAMA

I'll answer. Night night, baby.

ERIKA

Night night.

* * *

June 7th, 2011

Dear Ms. Erika Janie,

First of all, I was deeply touched by your birthday message. It really touched my heart. It was the most awesome message ever sent on my birthday! I too love you so very much. I will never forget my 1 million dollar birthday message from my precious Erika.

Make no mistake you are truly loved and cared about. That goes for your sister Samantha as well. There is so much more I wish to give and share with the two of you. I thank God so much for the both of you. (Especially you Erika!) You brought so much life, hope, and laughter into Samantha and my life from the first day (maybe the 7th day you were with us). A little tiny at first, but cute.

All I can say is that God is Good! When you are going through tough times first seek him out. (Read your Bible) and hold on to his promises. God (Jesus Christ) the Holy Spirit—They do not lie. Like we sometimes do or exaggerate the truth for whatever reasons.

I really enjoyed the 55 reasons for loving me (51-55-Powerful!) I shared them with a lady on the MARTA bus. We both enjoyed your expressions. I also

*shared them with my best girlfriend Janice, yes lord we
had a great time laughing. Erika, Thank You. Some
of the things you listed were so deep/sacred. You know
much about me as I do about you. I will always love you
sweetheart. I know the future for you will be awesome. The
reason(s) you recognize my greatness, courage, good, power,
gifts, etc—is because they are inside of you. And much
much and many more. Trust God and obey him and he
will give you and continue to bless you with FAVOR! You
are a miracle woman—was a miracle baby and is destined
for greatness!*

*Yes, I support your dreams and I probably dream with
you at times. You are remarkable, powerful, and forever
loved. Continue to bless those around you. And always
remember the joy of the Lord is your strength!*

Answers to some of your questions:

*41. How old was I when I had sex? 22. That's why I
married your daddy* ☺

*43. Can you remember your first kiss? Roy Gray—
He had really really big lips. Almost smothered me* ☺

44. What is the best gift a man has given you? His ♥
*Heart. Respect. Loyalty. Support unconditional. Love.
Forgiveness, when I acted a fool. Henry Orville Braddock*

45. "Worst" sexual encounter? Don't register ☺ *I am
careful, ok?*

*48. What turns you on? Sexy music by Barry White,
Marvin Gay, The Temptations. When naked with . . .
touching . . . All that. Middle appendage. Lips . . . lower. . . . . .*

49. What makes me feel sexy? Thoughts—Reality of connecting......

50. Yea yea......

Love Always,

MOM

Gift for you enclosed, Go Get em Tiger (EJ)
Career, Success, Love, Peace, Joy, Hope, Faith

December 17

Wake up.

What time is it? You have work at 6:55 am. You reach for your phone. It is 7:10. You do not react. You do not move to sit up. You rest your head against the warmth of the pillow and watch the sun glisten softly between the cracks in the blinds. Red is with you. He rubs his head against your feet, purring softly.

Your phone vibrates from beneath the pillow, right into the back of your skull. You let it vibrate two more times. It's Aunt Mattie. *Hm.*

"Hello."

"Hey, how you doing?"

"I'm late for work. I just woke up."

Your aunt Mattie does a soft, quick laugh. You know that something is different because she has a hard, forceful laugh. It's never been soft.

"That might be a good thing, darling. You might want to stay home today. *Be-cause*"—she pauses for only a beat, pushing forward, "the nurses at the hospice called. They say it's looking like she's gonna pass today." She does not say her name.

"What do you mean?" You are still facing the sun, the shards of light suddenly vulgar.

"She's been nonresponsive for about a week now, and they say her breathing has that rattle in it. When their breath gets hollow and has the rattling sound it usually means they're about to go." She sounds like she is leaning over the counter in her kitchen, probably fiddling with a dirty fork or the tie-string from the bread bag.

"Oh."

"They called and let us know in case we wanted to drive down and be there when she passes. I was thinking about heading out, but even if I leave now, by the time I get to Georgia it may be too late. I wish I could have—you know. If I had known I would have driven down this past weekend. But I'm glad I got to see her when I did. She was definitely looking like . . . But yeah. They say it'll probably be today."

You can't tell if she's freaking out. But you can't tell if you are either. "Okay."

"You may want to even call your job and let them know what the situation is so you don't get in trouble for being late or tardy or whatnot."

"Okay."

"Okay, darling. Stay by your phone. I'll let you know if I hear anything." *If she hears that your mother has passed away.*

"All right. Okay."

You place the phone back under your pillow and stare up at the ceiling. You do not call your job. You lie still. In this bed by yourself, nothing else exists. You are all alone in the world. Your mother is going to die today in a room with two or three strangers looking over her face. They call and tell you to expect it. Unreal. Death isn't supposed to announce itself. It's supposed to snatch you away quickly, so that you aren't waiting around all day for word. What an awful thing to wait for.

What do you do now? You can't go back to sleep. You'll have a dream you don't want to watch. These dreams scare you. She keeps appearing in them, on two good legs—never her from now. It's usually her from the early 2000s, when she was full of life and desire and her own little quirks. In voicemails she always says, "This is your mama. Sallie Simpson." Like you don't know her voice better than anything in the world. It's hilarious and you will never forget it.

You want to call your sister, but you are afraid to be calling with the news. Realistically, no one would call you first. Not for anything. You are too weepy and quiet. You don't brave it like your older sister or talk straight through it like your aunt. You skip ahead to the tragedy and let it consume. You relish the feeling of despair. You sink into it.

Samantha saw your mother twice after you. October and November. She said you wouldn't have been able to handle it and you believe her. It's pathetic that you couldn't afford to go back, but it was also a relief. Your sister said November almost broke her. She said Mama was paralyzed and couldn't walk anymore. She said her voice was long gone and that she had to mouth everything.

You never called her back after Thanksgiving. What if you're guilty of creating poetry for yourself? Writing scenes to cry over. You could have called her back. You knew that she would not feel better and so she would not call, and you left it there. Romantic tragedy.

Samantha said that one of the last conversations they shared was surreal. Your mother was in a good mood and told her that she got a phone call from President Barack Obama, who asked her to work for him as Head of Education in America. She said Mama sounded happy, so she congratulated her. Samantha has read books about dealing with death that suggested going along with any illusions the dying person is experiencing, because you shouldn't worry or stress them out with what's reality and what's not. You'd like the same treatment for the rest of your life.

You wonder if your mother is lying on that bed fully aware of everything that's happening. What if she is awake, listening to familiar strangers call her family to tell them that she will die today? You imagine them calling right beside the bed. Does she feel death slinking up her body? Will she welcome it?

You woke up feeling like you were exactly where you were supposed to be. Signs from the universe. You were meant to be at work according to a schedule your managers made up that said you would be needed on December 17 for the busy holiday season. The universe said no. It quieted your alarm. Let you rest. Woke you with the sun. This is exactly as the story was supposed to go, as it should have gone, as it will be told. The universe is a storyteller too. Your mother will pass today. You have been afraid for four months straight.

Aunt Linda Fae said the last time she spoke to her baby sister she said she was ready to come home. Linda Fae thought she meant heaven, but she really meant North Carolina for the holidays. After all of these years running from her family and toward success, she finally admitted that she wanted to go home. Of course by now it was too late. She wasn't well enough to ride in the backseat of a car for ten hours or go through airport security and the ordeal of flying. She had to stay. To see it through.

It's 9:00 am now. You've been staring at nothing for two hours when your phone vibrates in your hand. It's your sister. You want to spit up stomach bile onto the sheets. You want to release your bowels in between the covers. This is it.

"Hello?"

"Hi, Sister."

You both hold the phone for a beat too long. "Did you talk to Aunt Mattie already?"

"Yeah. The hospice called me. And then she called a little bit later." She pauses again.

You wonder how you ended up on the no call list. Though after freezing up with the nurses, you understand why. "They didn't call me. Aunt Mattie did. She told me that today may be the day."

"Yeah."

What more is there to say? She spoke last, so it's your turn. "I'm nervous."

"Me too."

"I missed work. By accident. And then Aunt Mattie called. It was weird."

"That is weird."

What else? You want to hang up, but you also want to hold the phone and listen to someone breathe. "I guess we have to wait now."

"Yeah." She sounds tense. Maybe she is crying her soft tears. She is so much softer than you. Her tears probably moisturize her skin. You remember how she looked when she cried underneath the streetlights after Mama kicked her out. Things were so different. You still have each other, even if you have nothing to say.

You decide it may be better to try to end the call. "I think I need to lay down some more."

"Okay. Yeah. I'll let you know if anything changes." She means she'll call you if they tell her first.

The trees sway in the rough Chicago wind outside your window. You watch their shadows dance furtively in front of the sun. It looks menacing to see the light fight through and be consumed by darkness again. The leaves, dry and brittle, rattle on their branches. You hear pieces of conversation passing on the sidewalk, but your room is bone quiet. The cat left a few minutes ago, bored with your unfriendly silence.

You try not to imagine your mama, but you have nothing else to think about. You pretend that she is packing her things. She's shuffling her paperwork and sliding it neatly into her book bag. She's folding her clothes and placing them in her suitcase. She's tucking the forty dollars into a hidden compartment in her wallet. She is readying herself for The Passing.

You picture a cure! She sits up with gasping breath, her eyes flying open. It's a miracle! The Lord has delivered her one more time. The doctors said she had two months, but now the cancer is gone. She's okay!

Your mind drifts back to reality at a dreadfully slow pace. You don't want to think anymore. You want to sleep, but sleeping is for people with peace of mind. You've heard her testimony all your life and now it's time for the verdict. You won't be able to sleep until you know. Let the universe be kind.

Your phone vibrates. A third and final time.

It's an email from Aunt Mattie. Just an email. The subject says: ***Mom's Passing.*** A prep email, probably:

> By now you both have received the news that your mom completed the transition today at 12:25 pm. You both have my condolences. By now most family have been notified. I fortunately didn't start the road trip this morning....would not have made it in time. Sis. Augustine says that they will hold your mom's things til next week so I guess I'll plan a trip to GA to get whatever she has there as well as clean out her storage....... before the weekend. As I am sure neither of you will be able to assist (not that I would ask), I'm gonna ask Chilita to help. I know there may be some important papers she may have wanted saved. I'll try to make a good judgment call on the rest. I can keep everything in Jr's building out back should either of you feel up to looking thru it this time around or some time in the future.
>
> The sun is shining beautifully here today. May God's peace warm all of our hearts as WE prepare for the last leg of this journey!
>
> Love You Both,
> Aunt Mattie

You read it again. *By now.* Wait. *By now you both have received the news that your mom completed the transition today.* Wait.

A small seed has fallen into the pit of your stomach, and it grows larger with every sentence. You don't understand. Why didn't someone call you? Why are you finding out like this? No, this is not the way the story ends. You do *not* read about it in an email!

You sit up in bed and dial your aunt Mattie's number. You can only focus on the smaller picture, the fact that you did not get the phone call that you have been waiting for since August.

"Hello?" Your aunt sounds tired but alert. She is being strong for you.

All the fight falls from your lips. She's doing the best she can. Her email said that she will drive down to Georgia and get the last of your mother's things. She will do all of that not for you, but for her sister. She sent an email because that was all she had left to offer after months of being the strong one. She thought you knew. That's all. She thought you knew.

"I didn't get a phone call."

"What do you mean?"

"No one told me Mama passed away. I found out from the email."

"Oh no. Oh, baby, I'm sorry. I thought they called everybody. I thought you were just trying to adjust so I sent an email. I'm sorry."

"It's okay." Maybe the email was the best possible outcome after all. "I've been afraid of the phone for months." You wondered for so long what the words would be.

Suddenly everything connects.

By now you know . . .

Your mother is dead.

Lamentations

~

Time doesn't move fast enough to heal. Everything is too present. The day Mama passed becomes the night Mama passed.

We played the Buffy board game. Chris, Shawn, Jeremy, and I. Jeremy was the first person I had to tell that she was gone. He'd been sleeping on the couch, his long legs dangling over the arm. I sat on the edge, startled him awake. Whispered the words. He lunged forward and hugged me tight. Tonight he played the villain—the Master vampire. I was Buffy. Good prevailed over Evil in a satisfying triumph. I ordered Giordano's deep dish and a side of wings and ate until my stomach hurt. Had sex. Drifted into blackness.

The next day Jeremy and I jumped into making our own web series—a mockumentary about us trying to get famous. Chris filmed our skits on his Nikon. Jeremy learned how to edit the clips together from a YouTube tutorial. I was creat-

ing something in Mama's name. One last effort to become who she saw me to be while her body was aboveground. We posted the videos online.

Nothing came of our efforts. But it distracted me from thinking of Mama's body for the whole week.

~

~

Mama's funeral is on Christmas Eve in North Carolina. The choir's bad. Half their voices crack during "Going Up Yonder," but I reckon the best singers are probably home with their families. They make Samantha and me close the casket. Is this a southern thing? Nobody warned us. We had to walk up to our mama's body and close the lid on her life. Women from Mama's high school basketball team came. Uncle Jit calls on them from the pulpit and they stand up one by one, old ladies on bad knees. I liked imagining them young and lanky. Running drills in jerseys with Mama. They gloss over her homelessness. Uncle Jit says she loved to do God's ministry in the streets. That's a way to put it.

A "perk" of grief is blatantly smoking cigarettes on Uncle Billy's front porch for the whole family to see. Nobody says shit to me. Uncle Frank nods when I come out. We bond in silence. Sharing his smoke spot by the garage. I can see the future. He'll be dead in five years. Uncle Billy in seven. Cousin Chilita, who helped Aunt Mattie pack up Mama's things, will be gone next year. Everyone will grieve.

Samantha and I spend Christmas Day with Aunt Mattie and Cousin Latrice and her babies. We sit on the sidelines. Watch our auntie be a grandma while the boys open gifts. A Temptations Christmas song begins to play from the den speakers, drifting over to the Christmas tree. "Silent Night." Mama's favorite. I lose it over the disgustingly merry nostalgia in the room. I run to the bathroom across the house. Sob uncontrollably over the sink, crying so hard I can't breathe. The door cracks open and my sister is there. No words. We hold each other on the fuzzy bath mat.

Later, the family sits around the television for the Doctor Who *Christmas special. He regenerates tonight. My sister and I sit silent, ears and eyes glazed over while the Doctor dies. Someone new replaces him in an instant after blinding light shoots from his limbs. We'll stop watching* Doctor Who *after tonight. Unsure why for years.*

~

~

I write everything down in my journal. The wake, the funeral, all the emotions of it. I carry the notebook with me everywhere, like my sister, scribbling in it incessantly, like Mama. Pages and pages of raw emotions I don't want to forget.

Chris invites me on a road trip from Chicago to Omaha. I'll see where he spent his teenage years and meet his parents. The jaunt to suburbia is jarring. We pull up to a nice home. His mother is kind, alive, has baby pictures ready to show. His father offers an occasional witty comment. It's normal. I'm painfully aware that I can never mirror this experience for him.

Chris drives us to a park and we walk along the edges of a lake. I'm thankful for a pensive moment. When we return to the car, the passenger window is broken out, glass scattered over the pavement. My purse has been stolen, my journal and its memories gone with it. I cry. It feels like a metaphor.

Back home in Chicago, Aunt Mattie asks if I've seen a small package from her in the mail yet. The packages at my building get stolen left and right, so I have everything come to me at the call center. She says she mailed me Mama's wallet, stuffed to the brim with cards and pictures behind her driver's license, and her glasses wrapped carefully in tissue paper. My heart drops to my stomach. She says she mailed it two weeks ago and was wondering why I hadn't said anything. It's been stolen. I'm sure of it. I'm at work, and I start crying so severely I have to leave early. Despite my questioning the neighbor and visiting the post office to beg someone to check the back room, the package is nowhere to be found. I'm heartbroken. What metaphor is this? What meaning?

~

~

DVDs Mama Owned That I Remember

- *Tyler Perry's Madea Goes to Jail* (play)
- *Tyler Perry's I Can Do Bad All by Myself* (play)
- *Ghost*
- *The Temptations*
- *A.I. Artificial Intelligence*
- *Black Knight*
- *Kingdom Come*
- *The Pursuit of Happyness*
- *K-PAX*
- *The Color Purple*
- *Forrest Gump*
- *Dreamgirls*

~

~

Initially, Mama is in most of my dreams. She doesn't do anything or say anything, but she's there. In one, she laughs beside me during hijinks with the cat. In a Marx Brothers–type dream, she shakes her head knowingly when we can't leave the hotel room. She lingers around me, until a dream that marks her last appearance: I am in my room and I hear her calling up to my window from downstairs, Jane! Jane! She smiles up at me when I pop my head out the second-floor window. She is her best self, somewhere around 2004, smiling up at me. I buzz her in.

We sit at a dining room table that doesn't exist in my apartment. Maybe the one we had in the house in North Carolina when I was three. We're laughing hysterically and when the cheer dies down Mama gets serious. I have something for you, she tells me. She pulls an envelope from her purse and pushes it toward me across the table. I have something for you, she says again. We give each other warm looks, and when I reach for the envelope I wake up.

A week later in the real world, Samantha receives a letter. Mama had a small insurance policy. We get seven thousand dollars to split. It isn't much, but she was able to leave us a little something after all. The first thing I do with the money is go to Joe's Crab Shack. Even though Mama doesn't visit my dreams anymore after that, I feel her presence around me often.

~

~

May 2014. My first Mother's Day without one. The endless Instagram posts of daughters and mothers make me nauseous. Life is unfair, and mostly to me. A coworker who lives nearby named Nadine and my upstairs neighbor Kat come over. It's an accident. Nadine is checking on me and Kat is looking for a cigarette. It just so happens that all our mothers are dead, and we laugh at our accidental Dead Mom Club meeting. We share a joint. It's a soothing moment.

A few days later, the need for a tattoo consumes me. I walk a block up the street and get Lucille Ball's face on my ankle, black traditional. I love Lucy. And not only that, my mother loved Lucy. It was her favorite show. She'd have it playing on the television for me at three years old. I've never laughed harder than at the bread flying out of the oven in an episode called "Pioneer Women."

Mama and I were both Lucy kinda ladies. Trapped in a domestic sphere. Fighting like hell to get out of it, to make it to the top, to Hollywood, to somewhere beyond the limitations of what others thought we could be. Leading with charm, ingenuity, and schemes. Demanding to be loved fully, entirely. A woman like Lucy sets a precedent, vibrates through time. That's how Mama was, to me. Unforgettable. Forever loved. Permanent in my skin.

~

~

The year has the nerve to pass. Samantha tells me to participate in National Novel Writing Month for November with her. She writes about time-traveling ladies in the South. All that comes out for me is a painful telling of Mama's death.

I need more happy memories.

~

~

Mama's Meds When They Released Her from the Mental Ward

- Risperdal—for schizophrenia, bipolar disorder, and autism spectrum, balances levels of dopamine and serotonin
- Klonopin—for panic attacks
- Metoprolol—for high blood pressure or treatment after heart attack
- Hydrochlorothiazide—for high blood pressure, water pill creates more urine
- Arimidex—used after tamoxifen, treats postmenopausal women after breast cancer

~

~

Mama didn't care for Buffy *or* Angel *too much, but she watched both shows because Samantha and I loved them. She'd irritate and amuse us with her mommy comments. She told Samantha not to hold her breath because* Buffy *was probably over after season five—"The girl is dead!"— which almost sent Samantha to tears. Mama said of* Angel, *"This show has everything. A vampire, a demon . . . and a nigguh!" She said both shows were predictable because they were stealing story lines from the Bible—which we would know if we had read it!*

After I left for college and she had the television to herself, she got into Ghost Whisperer. *She'd tell me about story lines over the phone or in email, and I'd grin at her excitement for the ghost lady. I never watched it, which I regret, but I gifted her the first couple seasons on DVD. I'm scared that if I try to watch it now, the absence of her commentary will destroy me.*

~

~

Samantha gets married to Damon amongst dinosaur bones at a museum in North Carolina. Mama can't be there, but Samantha makes sure her brothers and sisters can. Only Sallie Carol's daughter could have a wedding with an educational backdrop. I am glad Mama knew of Damon. I am glad she knew of Chris.

Meanwhile, Chris moves in with me and Shawn, making the rent a smooth $233 a person. The problem is that more white boys come after that, and then a tiki bar down the street, and then a modern remodel of the nineties Taco Bell, which means gentrification has come for us. The rent goes up to a thousand dollars at the same time the bedbugs come. We only leave because the landlord won't do anything about it. Admittedly, I brought in the bedbugs with a used mattress from Elan, but enough was enough. I stayed in my wooden Polish palace for seven years. Longer than any singular place I'd ever lived with Mama. Insane.

Like Mama, I start apartment hopping. Chris and I move into an attic unit that we learn is illegal after the fire department shows up for a carbon monoxide leak. Next we stay in an apartment the size of a tight hallway, and then Chris gets a job offer to move to San Francisco. I don't hesitate to go with him. I want to be anything other than what I have become: a southern girl selling Mod Podge lighters on Etsy out of her living room and crying about the past. I want a future. I wish my mother got one too. I hate how her story ended, and that I didn't move fast enough to change it. So I disappear into Chris' new journey, going along for the ride to the West Coast.

~

~

Mama's Various Degrees, Certificates, and Licenses

- Bachelor of Science, Cum Laude, Atlantic Christian College, 1978
- Master of Arts in Education, East Carolina University, 1986
- Georgia Educator Certificate, 1994–2004
- Certified Substance Abuse Prevention Consultant (CSAPC) License, 1995
- Master Addiction Counselor, American College, 1996/2005
- Certified Criminal Justice Specialist (CCJS), American College, 1996/2005
- License to Teach the Gospel, Body of Christ Ministry International, 2000
- Substance Abuse Correctional Setting Course, University of North Florida, 2001
- 43rd Annual Southeastern School of Alcohol and Other Drug Studies course, University of Georgia, 2003
- Certified Preventionist Level IV, Prevention Credentialing Consortium of Georgia, 2005
- Georgia Educator Certificate, 2005–2010
- Certificate of Advanced Graduate Studies in Educational Leadership, Cambridge College, 2006
- Alcohol & Drug Risk Reduction, 2008
- DUI Instructor Certification, 2008/2012

~

~

I shake bubble tea in Chinatown, San Francisco, and pretend I don't want to act and don't know how to write. Mama would have hated it. Another year passes. I decide to apply to graduate school to make her happy and use chunks of the Mama writings I did the previous November as sample words. The University of San Francisco accepts me immediately. Dopamine courses through my veins in a way I haven't felt in a long time. Feeling bold, I ask them if I can study both fiction and nonfiction. They tell me it's not something they do. I send a sample of my fiction writing. They say never mind, they'll figure out a way for me to do both. I am my mother's daughter! Elated until I see the price of tuition. They offer a little scholarship money, but I'd still need ten thousand more.

This freezes me in my tracks. Mama would have called the financial aid office and got a woman she could sway on the line. Given them a testimony so moving they'd add an extra zero at the end of my offer. But Mama isn't here. I don't go.

Another year passes. I miss her endlessly, daily. She was the sun and I rotated around her. How does the Earth keep spinning on its axis?

~

Aloha

The second my feet step from the jetway into Hartsfield-Jackson Atlanta International Airport, I'm nauseous. It's 2018. I haven't been to Georgia since Mama was here. Only Zavieta's Dirty Thirty weekend could get me back.

Ellen picks me up from Arrivals with the same energy she had when we were sixteen, whipping around the corner blasting Gorilla Zoe at 7:30 in the morning before school. It's a weird sensation to be back where you came from but unsure where to go.

We visit my godkids at their elementary school. I haven't seen them since they were toddlers in a grainy photo with my mother at hospice. The last babies she saw. They're taller now. The top of Lil Charles' head comes up to my breasts, and he grins like a boy who appreciates breasts already. Makayla's toddler body has formed into a gymnast girl with strong legs. They both smile up at me expectantly, call me Auntie, make me feel like so much time has passed. I don't disappoint, pulling out key chains with their names on them, Pocky sticks, and a baggy of Asian candies from Chinatown. Their excitement makes me giddy. I am careful not to promise I'll see them again. Only maybes. They hug me tight, scurry back to class.

Atlanta is so sprawling we spend half an hour in the car for every stop we make. Ellen has to work reception for a couple hours at a massage business to supplement her own mobile massage business. It reminds me of Mama's hustle. A lady comes in selling bracelets for a dollar and ends up debating the merits of voting with Ellen. The lady says, "They ain't counting our votes anyway. The government will let us all die. Change starts in your community." We can all agree with that. She heads to the next office in the strip mall with her bracelets.

We grab lunch at American Deli. I feel at home with every crunch of perfectly coated chicken wing. We hit up the members of Le Entourage, my high school girl gang, and agree to meet at Krystal's house.

With my girlhood crew, it only takes a moment to warm up. We have drinks and blunts and laugh our asses off trying to remember the rap verses we wrote a decade ago. No one talks about careers or the future, thank God. Everyone's impressed enough that I live in California. We only talk about the fun parts of the past, celebrity gossip, our old classmates' juicy tea. They sprinkle in a few memories of my mama shuffling through the hallways of the high school to work with our principal. I'm glowing inside. Hearing her alive.

It's one in the morning. Ellen and I hug the girls, kiss Krystal's twin babies good night, and head back to the car. I'm tired in a way that feels like thirty creeping up on me. Ellen starts the engine and winks from the driver's seat. She says she has a surprise.

She knows her studio apartment is cramped and half an hour away, so she's gotten us a hotel room for the night. "*Cute!*"

I respond. Laughing that we sound like lovers. That we're adults who grab hotel rooms just to feel alive. When I fuss at her for the splurge, she assures me she didn't spend too much. It's a quickie kinda room, she says, nothing major, just somewhere to be.

She's driving with one hand and reading texts with another—flirting with a mister. We exit the highway, and then we're coasting down Memorial Drive. I take a deep breath in and out as we pass the Publix my mother walked to so often, her post office and T.J. Maxx, the Chinese Buffet my sister and I ate at every time she got paid from her mall job.

Some stores have changed, but the buildings hold their secrets. You can always tell a Pizza Hut's a Pizza Hut, no matter what name they slap on the front. You can't change the foundation. The car slows at the same moment I am hoping it will speed up.

Ellen pulls into a place that twists my stomach into knots. America's Best Value. The sign colors are blue, but I know they used to be burgundy. I wouldn't forget this building, its old name: Aloha Motor Inn. A pressure builds in my head. I want her to keep driving, merge onto the highway, and speed until we leave the city. I want miles and state lines between myself and this facility. My ears refocus. Ellen sounds like she's been here before. I'm not sure how to tell her I have too.

I peed the bed with my mama and sister sleeping in it at Aloha Motor Inn. We lived there—here—when I was in fifth grade. The toilet was only four feet from the queen-size bed we shared, but the darkness was massive. This was my least favorite type of motel, flat one-levels where the rooms sit directly on the parking lot. The outside right behind the curtains. Men in sagging jeans and oversized T-shirts roamed around at night like roaches beneath a trash can, hovering together or scattering at the flash of light. There was barely any, save for the orange glow from a single streetlamp on the sidewalk.

Ellen comes back from the lobby office with the key. As we get our things from the car and walk inside, two men watch, smoking their cigarettes in the shadows. My heart hammers as Ellen taps the key card against the door.

Aloha was where I discovered *The X-Files*. Something darker after *The Simpsons*. Mulder and Scully's basement office was home to me. They made me feel brave. This wasn't a show for kids. There were monsters in the vents and aliens in labs. They showed real stuff too, like killer cockroaches and a corrupt government. Theirs was a darkness I felt comfortable inside.

Season four, episode two, "Home." Mulder and Scully investigate a recluse family after a deformed baby is found buried in a field. The family consists of three mutated brothers with a secret: not only are they inbred; they mate with their quadruple amputee mother, who they keep hidden under the bed on a sliding slab. My tiny eyes could have popped out of my head. My family had secrets but nothing like that! There were so many different types of scary. I never pissed the bed again.

Ellen pushes open the door. I'm afraid to look up from the handle of my suitcase. The carpet is that same busy vomit-inducing pattern, designed to hide stains. The tropical wallpaper is gone thank God, the room now an off-off-off-white color, and it smells like the ghost of a cigarette, despite the nonsmoking signs. The bed sits pathetically in the middle of the room waiting for us. I'm going to pass out.

Ellen reaches behind me to close the door and set the flimsy chain lock. She plops down on the flower-patterned bedspread with a look of contentment on her face. She unloads her purse and overnight bag onto the bed and leans back into the pillows to check her social media. My teeth are clenched tight. I can almost see my eight-year-old self, sitting cross-legged on the floor in front of the bed, trying to focus on the television. Nothing else but the television as Mama calls her sister on a prepaid phone, pleading for seventy dollars for the room fee.

I don't smoke cigarettes anymore, but I can tear down a blunt. I must refuse to be afraid. Otherwise this room will kill me.

America's Best Value. They were bold to name it that. There's nothing worth anything here. Aloha made more sense. Hello and goodbye. Get in and get the hell out as soon as your money's right. I use a piece of paper from my journal to catch the weed I grind down with my fingers. I feel as ghetto as the hotel. This is who I really am, inside these walls. The parts of me I'd been burying since I took off north for a better life in Chicago.

Ellen is already on the phone, one leg swung over the other as she talks to a deep voice. I stand up to throw away my blunt wrapper and smack her ass playfully on my way back, trying to seem casual. She sticks her tongue out at me. Twerks in my direction, entirely unaware that I am dying. I sprinkle weed into the wrap, pat it down.

She asks if he wants to come over. I roll my eyes. She could never just do girls night. "How far away are you?" she whispers into the phone. I lick my blunt wrap closed and motion that I'm going outside. I remember being afraid of the guys who hung around the parking lot at the hotels and apartments where we stayed. I imagined them breaking in and touching us. Now I'm one of them.

Underneath the same orange glow that kept my window from going dark when I was little, I light my blunt. Inhale deep. Imagine I'm the Cigarette Smoking Man from *The X-Files*, stepping away from a government secret, leaving the catastrophe stowed away in a room. Exhale.

One of the two men who were loitering when we checked in is still standing across the lot. Our eyes connect. I try to avert my gaze slowly, offer no invitation. He flicks his cigarette away, starts walking toward me like I waved him over. The streets around us are pitch-black and empty.

I remind myself that I am not scared. That black men aren't monsters, just victims of a white perception that can turn innocent brown boys into nightmares. The man slides up to stand beside me, white tee and sagging acid jeans. I keep staring forward. Unsure how friendly to be, I inhale deep on my blunt. He sways forward so his face is in my vision and flashes his teeth at me, then asks for a lighter. Somehow parking lot men always need a lighter even though they were just smoking. I remain wordless, hand him my lime green Bic. He pulls a half-smoked cigarette from somewhere and looks me up and down. "You from around here?"

I try to answer without hesitation or fear. "Yup, Decatur where it's greater." I throw in that I live in California now and I'm only in town for a birthday. I'm doing that humanizing thing with my details. Not that he's a killer. I see his friend across the parking lot now, lighting another cigarette as he watches everything. They could be sex traffickers.

"You don't sound like you from here. . . ." He's analyzing my voice in a way that makes me feel like I'm in middle school again. He thinks he's made me. I am mad and for a moment forget my fears, "I am from here, *right here*; I literally used to live in this goddamn motel." I inhale and exhale and refuse to look him in the eye. I haven't even told Ellen, but I'm telling this man. I'm claiming it out loud, proudly.

He could take offense at my tone. It's too quiet out here for raised voices. He stares at me for a beat before chuckling and returning my lighter. I hold my blunt in his direction, a peace offering. He takes a long drag, exhales, passes it back. Hits his cigarette. After I offer no further hits or conversation, he tells me to be easy and goes back over to his friend.

I inhale once more. Exhale long and slow. I wonder how many kids are behind the rows of curtains in this flat-level motel, how many families. I wish them peace through the night.

I put the smoke out. Fumble with the key card to get back into our room. Ellen's laughing in the dark. She tells her mister to come before 2:00 am if he's really about it. I sink onto the bed and try to get lost in my phone before feigning sleep. I'm under only the top comforter with my clothes still on and my arms crossed, wishing I was tucked in between those two warm bodies that kept me safe, that understood the darkness. I hear Ellen slipping out of bed, creeping toward the door, undoing the chain, and slipping out.

It feels impossible to sleep, but before I know it, I'm opening my eyes to sunlight, both hands pressed between my thighs. For a moment, my mother's voice floats to my ears, halfway through a story. But that's not right. Ellen is beside me in bed, laughing on the phone with her sister. It's been twenty years and one night. I survived.

Later that evening, we celebrate Zavieta. She's having a hotel party of all things. The two of us spent the day picking up wing trays and hanging decorations in the suite she rented downtown. We reminisce about Sour Skittle palms, notes folded into triangles, and childhood crushes. I meet Zavieta's boyfriend and reunite with her brother's ex-wife Jatana, who raised her. Jatana mentions my mama, how proud she'd be that I made it to California and how much that lady could talk. This makes me laugh.

There's a Shirley Caesar song, "I Remember Mama," where she croons about her departed mother. Mama used to play that song out. She said one day we'd really understand it: Shirley sang about growing up with holes in her shoes, and how the Lord saw them through, and that her mama was the glue that kept the family together. "I remember Mama in a happy way," she sang.

I have to try to do the same.

Zavieta blows out the candles on her thirtieth-birthday cake. The room is filled with joyful voices. I take a moment to stare out the tall windows of the hotel room, overlooking the bright lights of Mama's favorite city. Cheers.

Book of Sallie Carol 6:12: There are no neat, happy endings, only the next step in the journey.

On the way to the airport, you'll reflect and release. You had fun with your girls, with people who knew you, knew your mother. All of you still growing and becoming. You'll carry this good energy back to the West Coast and use it to feel more alive. Jeremy will call with good news—his play is going to Off Broadway. He'll encourage you to try graduate school again. You'll recognize that he's a Gemini sun and Taurus moon just like your mother, and you will heed his education advice. This time, the scholarships work out. You'll excel in school. And you'll excel beyond.

*   *   *

June 2023

I stop writing, shaking my head at my past self. I press "Sam!" from the favorites menu on my cell phone and listen to it ring. When I was little, Samantha told me I could call her Sam when we were the same age, and I nodded vigorously, taking it entirely to heart. I'm still waiting for the eight-year age gap to close. The contact name isn't what I call her, but a quote from Supernatural, *during our Tumblr days, when we were obsessed with the handsome spooky brothers, carrying on the family business. We actually call each other Shirley, from a joke we had with Shani about how all old black ladies are named some form of Cheryl.*

"Hello?" Samantha finally answers.

"Hey, Sister."

"Hey, Sister."

"Did I tell you about when I went back to Atlanta for Zavieta's thirtieth birthday and Ellen took me to Aloha to spend the night?"

"What!" she shouts in that perfect tone of disbelief and amusement.

"Yes!"

"Aloha Motor Inn?"

"Yes!"

"Wait, did you tell Ellen about our history with the place?"

"No! I didn't say a word! I think I emotionally blacked out."

"Shirley!" she says, this time disbelief mixed with empathy. "You better get into therapy; it does wonders."

"Yeah, yeah. Why can't I just mooch off what the lady tells you?" We laugh, and a playful shriek comes from Samantha's background, my niece, almost three years old. Our darling. Born in June like our mama but a Cancer like Auntie Erika. She loves books, being friendly with strangers—to my sister's mortification—and is as obsessed with Halloween as we are. (Never Christmas, only Halloween!) She is the next generation. Playing teacher in her room, mirroring her mama and grandma. Growing up in a stable home with a father and mother and surrounded by love.

"Are you coming for your birthday?" my sister asks.

I tell her it's highly possible. She says the birthday hat is waiting for me. It's over a decade old now, the felt material peeling all over, and the crown shape leaning forward. Outside of 2020, we've spent every birthday together. We have hours-long conversations on WhatsApp as often as possible. We read romance novels together and text about the steamy parts. We have inside jokes and matching pop culture T-shirts, and can't fight for more than an hour. We have each other, still. Mama's fondest wish.

*   *   *

There's a tunnel in downtown Atlanta with glowing orange lights along the sides. It feels like home to drive through it at night. I am safe and dozing off in the passenger seat as the lights pass by. I feel my mama beside my shoulder, focused on the road. I can hear her voice. Her humming.

She's in all our boyish memories, fussing and telling her stories and dropping us off at the next location. She is almost visible on the streets of Memorial Drive, her white sneakers making their way past the laundromat and the Jamaican café, and onward to the post office beside Publix.

She is just down the street again, at the house we had when things were good, scribbling in her spiral notebooks until the cats yawn that they are sleepy and I make it home safe.

I can sit in a booth at Waffle House, taste my youth in a cup of sweet tea, right across from where she sat, gossiping on the phone with a friend.

I could almost call Mama and ask where she has gone, what she is doing. I could almost get an answer.

Voicemail, July 11, 2013, 4:32 pm

"Hey, baby, this is your mama, Sallie Simpson. I just wanted to give you a call and hear your beautiful voice. I hope whatever you're doing you're having fun. I want you to have a good time, okay? Don't you worry about me. I'm doing just fine. You just stay focused on your work and achieving those dreams. And have faith in God. Always remember how good God has been to you. Anyway, give me a call later, all right? I love you! You know I love you, baby girl. Bye-bye."

Acknowledgments

Jeremy O. Harris, your birth is my birth; your death is my death. Without you this could not have come to fruition.

Christopher Rubarth, my love, my Lala, thank you for keeping us afloat while I sank into the past.

Aunt Mattie, thank you for absolutely everything. Your sister would be so proud you kept your promise.

My sister, Samantha Novella (I got one more thing!), thank you for keeping your last name. Simpson sisters forever.

My editor Emily Polson, as always, thank you for your mind, for seeing the vision.

My literary agent, Cindy Uh, thank you for fighting for me as hard as Mama would.

Berry and Novella Parker, my mama's deceased parents, her other siblings, living and watching over: Bertha, Vernell, Berry Jr., Linda Fae, Raymond, Jerry, Bruce Wayne, and Patricia. This is your daughter, your sister.

Sallie Carol Parker Simpson, we say your name.

Thank you for reading.

About the Author

Erika J. Simpson is a southern girl living in Denver, Colorado, with her partner and their little black cat. She holds an MFA in creative writing from the University of Kentucky, which awarded her the 2021 MFA Award in Nonfiction. Her essay "If You Ever Find Yourself" was published in Roxane Gay's *The Audacity* and featured in *The Best American Essays 2022*, edited by Alexander Chee. *This Is Your Mother* is her debut memoir, and she also writes fiction for the page and screen.